THE MAGICAL LIFE OF LONG TACK SAM

ANN MARIE FLEMING

RIVERHEAD BOOKS
Published by the Penguin Group
Penguin Group (USA) Inc.
375 Hudson Street, New York, New York 10014, USA

Penguin Group (Canada), 90 Eglinton Avenue East, Suite 700, Toronto, Ontario M4P 2Y3, Canada
(a division of Pearson Penguin Canada Inc.)
Penguin Books Ltd., 80 Strand, London WC2R 0RL, England
Penguin Group Ireland, 25 St. Stephen's Green, Dublin 2, Ireland (a division of Penguin Books Ltd.)
Penguin Group (Australia), 250 Camberwell Road, Camberwell, Victoria 3124, Australia
(a division of Pearson Australia Group Pty. Ltd.)
Penguin Books India Pvt. Ltd., 11 Community Centre, Panchsheel Park, New Delhi—110 017, India
Penguin Group (NZ), 67 Apollo Drive, Rosedale, North Shore 0745, Auckland, New Zealand
(a division of Pearson New Zealand Ltd.)
Penguin Books (South Africa) (Pty.) Ltd., 24 Sturdee Avenue, Rosebank, Johannesburg 2196, South Africa
Penguin Books Ltd., Registered Offices: 80 Strand, London WC2R 0RL, England

The publisher does not have any control over and does not take responsibility for author or third-party
websites or their content.

First Riverhead trade paperback edition: September 2007

Library of Congress Cataloging-in-Publication Data

Fleming, Ann Marie.
The magical life of Long Tack Sam / Ann Marie Fleming.
p. cm.
ISBN: 978-1-59448-264-9
1. Long Tack Sam, 1885-1961—Comic books, strips, etc.
2. Magicians—China—Biography—Comic books, strips, etc.
GV1545.L66 F44   2007   2007060352
793.8092 B 22

Printed in the United States of America

10 9 8 7 6 5 4 3 2 1

for my grandmother, Mina
with love

THE MAGICAL LIFE OF LONG TACK SAM

HI. MY NAME IS ANN MARIE FLEMING.

I'VE GOT A VERY INTERESTING STORY TO TELL YOU ABOUT MY GREAT-GRANDFATHER, LONG TACK SAM.

BUT FIRST I HAVE TO TELL YOU SOME THINGS ABOUT MYSELF. BEAR WITH ME.

I WAS BORN IN NAHA, OKINAWA, IN 1962...

WAAH!

Okinawa is a small island at the end of the southern-most tip of the Japanese archipelago.

*Okinawa was a United Nations dependency then, not actually part of Japan.

BIG BABY

I was a lot bigger than the other Japanese babies in the maternity ward.

Maybe that's because my father was a tall Australian.

My mother was from Hong Kong, and not very tall at all.

If your parents weren't Japanese, you couldn't get a birth certificate (unless you were born on the U.S. base, like most foreigners were).

KOREA

Ann Marie Fleming
born: Jul 29
weight: 8 lb.

my footprints

The closest country that would give me a birth certificate was Korea.

WAAH!

I couldn't leave the country because you needed an exit visa, and you need an entry visa to get an exit visa, and I didn't have an entry visa because I was born there.

GO FIGURE.

We went to Australia... (my father's home). No jobs.

We went to Hong Kong (my mother's home). My brother was born here.

...and landed up in Vancouver, where we stayed for a while. I became a Canadian citizen when I was 12. Because my parents did.

I grew up there.

I'm a filmmaker, amongst other things. And this is how it happened. I had always grown up with cameras, but art was a hobby (an immigrant thing).

I WAS VERY CLOSE TO MY MATERNAL GRANDMOTHER, MINA... BUT SHE DIED A LONG TIME AGO...

GRANNY LIKED TO SING AND DANCE BUT DIDN'T GIVE MANY DETAILS AND THERE WEREN'T ANY PICTURES, EITHER. MAYBE BECAUSE THEY WERE DESTROYED DURING THE WAR IN HONG KONG.

NO ONE WAS VERY INTERESTED.

She was half Austrian and used to talk about being Eurasian and her old Vaudeville days assisting in her dad's magic act. She talked about playing the theatre circuit, her celebrity friendships, and this tiki she got from a Maori Princess.

ANYWAY, I JUST THOUGHT OF HER AS MY GRANDMOTHER... UNTIL SHE DIED... AND THEN I COULDN'T STOP THINKING ABOUT HER STORIES... AND MY OWN...

KIND OF A "WHERE DO WE COME FROM? WHAT ARE WE? WHERE ARE WE GOING?" KIND OF THING.

*apologies to Paul Gauguin

I was in art school, studying animation, but I couldn't draw very well...

I PREFERRED USING A LIVE-ACTION CAMERA AND MADE A FILM ABOUT MY RELATIONSHIP WITH MY GRANDMOTHER AND WHAT I KNEW ABOUT HER. IT WAS AN EXPERIMENTAL FILM CALLED "WAVING" AND IT WAS 7 MINUTES LONG.

*"Waving" references Stevie Smith's poem, "Not Waving But Drowning"

AMF under water -->>

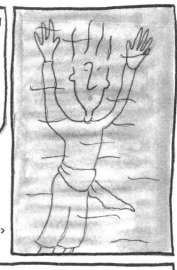

BUT THEN, I WAS RUN OVER BY A COUPLE OF CARS, AND COULDN'T WALK OR SHOOT ANYTHING. (I FELT VERY TIRED AND "RUN DOWN".)

ALL I COULD DO WAS DRAW, AND I MADE UP A CHARACTER...

"STICKGIRL"
WHO ACTS OUT ALL MY STORIES

me, AMF

I'M ALWAYS MAKING FILMS ABOUT MY FAMILY, TRYING TO FIGURE THEM OUT... BUT NOBODY KNOWS ANYTHING ABOUT MY GRANDMOTHER'S LIFE... OR HER FAMILY'S... EXCEPT

someone was crazy

someone was rich

someone was mean...

4

BUT I FOUND THESE STORIES VERY INTERESTING. WHY DID EVERYONE IN MY FAMILY LIVE ALL AROUND THE WORLD? WHY DIDN'T PEOPLE TALK TO EACH OTHER?

EVERYBODY FOUGHT

We found some old 16mm film in my grandparents' basement

It smelled like vinegar and was crispy and falling apart...

SAL DRE

I had inherited an old projector from my grandfather, and when I screened the film...

There she was... my young, beautiful grandmother, in New Zealand (with the Maori Princess), in Austria, Australia, Brazil, Germany with her...

...very handsome father...

LONG TACK SAM

5

WITH HIS NAME...

BIG

IN LIGHTS
(in different languages)

ON MARQUEES

PRINCE OF WALES THEATRE
AUCKLAND, NEW ZEALAND

...ALL OVER THE WORLD...

All I knew about him was that he was a magician, and could make coins appear from behind your ear.

I thought the film might have some value for an Asian American historical archive or something...

But no one had the resources to take care of it.

I had just finished an artist's residency in Germany* in a castle, my family had left Canada and I had nowhere to live and no job. I didn't know what to do with the film.

*Actually, living in Germany was pretty interesting because I had to learn a new language. And when I wanted to stay, it was hard to renew my visa, so I got a good lesson on what it is like to be an immigrant, as an adult. It's different!

While I was visiting Toronto, a friend took me, with his son, to see an old-time magic show at the Royal Ontario Museum by magician David Ben.
David Ben's son played hockey with the son of another friend of mine, documentarian Ron Mann, who told him about my footage. David Ben had heard of Long Tack Sam. Coincidence?

"THE CONJUROR"

He picked a piece of lint off my knee. (Magicians are very particular.)

David Ben told me about a magic collector's conference in Schaumburg, Illinois, just out by the Chicago airport. I went...

←I took my video camera everywhere

...just by ANOTHER coincidence, I was going to visit my new boyfriend, Bruce, there... AND...

The National Film Board of Canada had given me some $$$ to research my great-grandfather's story, so I could afford to go...

THE CONFERENCE
It was filled with books and tricks and magicians and collections and historians and magic fans...

All I had was this playbill from a theatre in Germany that Long Tack Sam had performed at from 1933.

Carl, an Austrian magician, hadn't heard of him but told me the "SCALA" still existed...

but it showed only exotic dancers now...

then, someone led me down an aisle, past all this magic paraphernalia...

People wanted pictures of me standing with my relatives.

There, on the far wall, with posters of Houdini and Blackstone, was my grandmother and her sister, in full Chinese dress. I had no idea.

I have to say, it was very emotional.

Me, with short hair.

I was introduced to magician Jay Marshall*, who had met Long Tack Sam and said there was something in a book about him...

*Jay Marshall is known as the "Dean of American Magicians"

...in *Quicker Than the Eye*, by John Mulholland.*

*John Mulholland was a good friend of Long Tack Sam and always tried to promote him. But the story he told sounded crazy.

There he was, in a drawing by Cyrus Leroy Baldridge, Doing the ancient Chinese magic trick "The Goldfish Bowl."
There was an entire chapter dedicated to him and Chinese magic.

Now, we are not a very Chinesey family, and the only pictures I had ever seen of Long Tack Sam were of him in Western clothes. I just thought of him as my great-grandfather, not as a particularly "Chinese Guy." "Cosmopolitan," I guess you'd call it. A citizen of the world. He was very short and carried a big cigar.

I knew he lived in New York City and knew Jack Benny and Walt Disney and Cary Grant and Laurel and Hardy and George Burns.
And I thought, "Neat, but big deal." It wasn't like that had anything to do with my life. And it was all a long, long time ago.

I had always been interested in magic, (I can do some party tricks) but I didn't know anything about that world, and suddenly, I'm introduced to all these magicians, who want to help me find the history of my great-grandfather, and their own history before it slips away.

In the Year of the Rabbit I go to New York City to do more research. Stanley Palm, a magician I met at the conference, lives there.

He is curious as to where all the $$$ went.

Stanley is sure there will be material about Long Tack Sam in the Billy Rose Theatre Collection of the New York Public Library at Lincoln Center.

? WHAT ?
MONEY

And I met Mark Mitton, another magician, who was researching Max Malini, a magician who was friends with LONG TACK SAM.

Mark said he worked with Chinese acrobats who might have heard of Long Tack Sam because all Chinese magicians come from the world of acrobatics.

REALLY?

First I didn't know he did a Chinese magic act. Now, he's an acrobat! Wild.

LONG TACK SAM (seated, center) and troupe - circa 1915

Stanley Palm took me to the apartment of Maureen Christopher, keeper of the Milbourne Christopher Magic Collection. Maureen showed me an interview Long Tack Sam did for a paper in NYC in 1915. This is how he described his rags-to-riches story. Right from the horse's mouth! So, it must be true, right?
We did it up in the style of the golden age of comics.
(These were drawn by Julian Lawrence.)

"WHEN I WAS FIVE YEARS OLD, FAMINE CAME TO OUR NORTH CHINESE COUNTRY. WE WERE HUNGRY AND MISERABLE.

A MAGICIAN CAME WORKING MIRACLES--

HE WAS A FAMOUS FRIEND OF THE SPIRITS.

HIS NAME WAS WANG.

HE COULD TAKE NEEDLES OUT OF HIS MOUTH FOR HALF AN HOUR AT A TIME.

HE COULD MAKE BEAUTIFUL VASES APPEAR IN THE MIDDLE OF THE DOOR.

HE COULD PERFORM A HUNDRED MAGIC FEATS.

I SAID TO MYSELF:

SURELY HE CAN TURN STONES INTO BREAD!

I WENT AND BOWED BEFORE THE MAGICIAN WANG AND TOLD HIM I WAS HUNGRY, AND BEGGED HIM TO MAKE BREAD FOR ME.

HE SQUATTED IN THE PUBLIC SQUARE AND REPLIED THAT THERE WERE MARVELS THAT THE SPIRITS WOULD ALLOW TO BE WORKED ONLY BEFORE ADEPTS.

HE SOMETIMES PERFORMED THE MYSTERIOUS AND TERRIBLE RITE OF CONJURING BREAD--

BUT ONLY IN THE PRESENCE OF HIS PUPILS OR OF WIZARDS OF HIGH DEGREE.

I BEGGED HIM TO TAKE ME AS ONE OF HIS PUPILS.

HE AGREED, AND HAD ME TAKE HIM TO MY PARENTS.

THEY GLADLY BOUND ME OVER TO SO GREAT A MAN IN SO WONDROUS A PROFESSION.

WANG TAUGHT ME THE ARTS OF CHINESE NECRO-MANCY. THE CHINESE MAGICIAN UNDERGOES LONG AND ARDUOUS TRAINING.

HE BEGINS AS A CHILD--

--AND STUDIES UNTIL HE HAS REACHED MANHOOD AND ADEPTHOOD.

AND THEN HE SALLIES FORTH--

AND DISPLAYS HIS CERTIFICATE OF GRADUATION AND WORKS HIS ART ON STREET CORNERS--

IN THE POPULAR THEATRES--

AND IN THE PALACES OF THE MANDARINS.

UPON MY GRADUATION I JOINED A WESTERN CIRCUS PERFORMING IN CHINA--

--AND WHEN THEY RETURNED TO THE OCCIDENT I WENT WITH THEM.

I DID NOT SEE CHINA AGAIN FOR TWENTY YEARS."

WHAT HAPPENS NEXT? WHERE WILL LONG GO? WHO WILL HE MEET? FIND OUT NEXT MONTH IN

Magical COMICS & STORIES

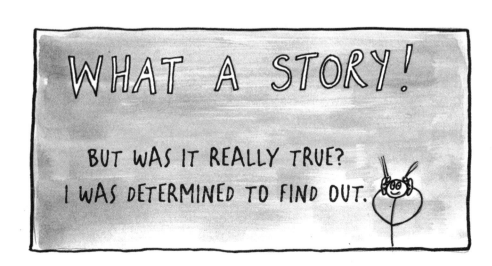

WHAT A STORY!

BUT WAS IT REALLY TRUE? I WAS DETERMINED TO FIND OUT.

To paraphrase the great, mixed-race bard, Bob Marley, you have to know where you come from so you can know where you're going to.
I come from a restless family.
And we are not so much in touch. But I need their help to find out more.

AUSTRIA OR BUST!

After Sam left China, I heard he went to America and I heard he went to England. I went to Austria because I knew he married my great-grandmother there, in 1908.

Ybbs. Donaulinde

Sam and his group of artists are invited to perform at the Coliseum in Linz

This is the village she comes from.

I went to talk to an old neighbor of the family's, my grandmother's childhood sweetheart, Ernst Kriechbaum. This is what he told me.

WHILE ON A EUROPEAN TOUR, LONG DID SOME SHOPPING AT A DEPARTMENT STORE IN LINZ, AUSTRIA

Esterman

WHILE PURCHASING SOAP AND TOOTHPASTE HE MET THE SHOPGIRL LEOPOLDINE ROESLER.

THEY SOON FELL IN LOVE --

POLDI-- JA--?

WILL YOU MARRY ME?

JA!!

IS THAT ROMANTIC OR WHAT?

IF I HADN'T SPENT THE PAST 2 YEARS IN GERMANY LEARNING THE LANGUAGE...

I WOULDN'T BE ABLE TO TALK WITH ERNST... I WOULDN'T HAVE FOUND THIS STORY

THIS IS POLDI...

...THIS IS SAM...

WHAT WERE THEY THINKING?

18

SAM PROPOSED, THEN WAS OFF TO BUDAPEST, HUNGARY, WITH HIS TROUPE, WRITING POLDI LOVE LETTERS IN BROKEN GERMAN...

THE
TAN-KWAI'S
Original
❀ Chinese Troupe. ❀

Conjurers, Contortionists
and
Jugglers, Acrobats, &c.

American Park
B U D A P E S T.
15. August 1902.   190

Mein Lieber Poldi.

*MY DEAREST POLDI, I HAVE ALREADY WRITTEN YOU TWO LETTERS AND HAVE RECEIVED NO RESPONSE. WHY HAVEN'T YOU ANSWERED ME? PLEASE WRITE IMMEDIATELY AND SEND PICTURES FROM WHEN WE WERE LAST TOGETHER IN LINZ. I MEAN THE PICTURE WHEN WE WERE BOTH IN YOUR HOME TOWN. MY DEAR POLDI, I HOPE YOU WILL WRITE SOON AND SEND ME PICTURES. MY BEST TO YOUR MOTHER (FRAU ROESLER). ALSO, MY LOVE TO YOU POLDI. I SEND YOU ENDLESS KISSES. SAM

MINA
VANCOUVER, 1987

I KNEW ABOUT THEIR WEDDING FROM MY GRANDMOTHER, MINA, WHO HAD KEPT THE FRONT PAGE OF THE ARTICLE THAT APPEARED IN A VIENNA NEWSPAPER. I THINK IT MADE EVERY NEWSPAPER IN AUSTRIA...

IT WAS SO STRANGE!

19

SAM, WHO WAS A BUDDHIST, BECAME A ROMAN CATHOLIC TO MARRY POLDI.

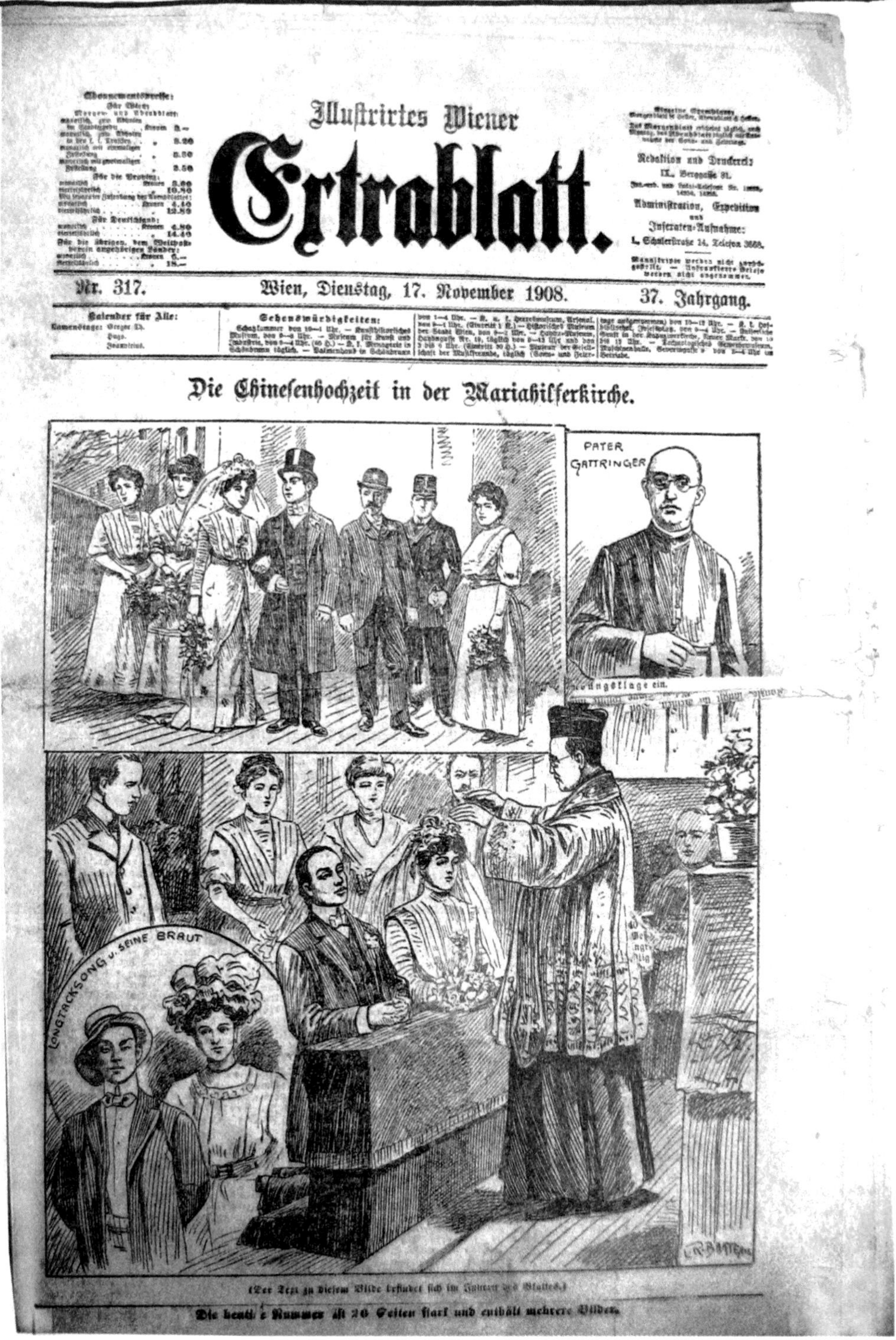

Illustrirtes Wiener
Extrablatt.
Redaktion und Druckerei:
Administration, Expedition
und
Inseraten-Aufnahme:
Nr. 317.
Wien, Dienstag, 17. November 1908.
37. Jahrgang.
Kalender für Alle:
Sehenswürdigkeiten:
Die Chinesenhochzeit in der Mariahilferkirche.
PATER GATTRINGER
LONGTACKSONG u. SEINE BRAUT
Die heuti e Nummer ist 26 Seiten stark und enthält mehrere Bilder.

Wasn't it strange in 1908 for a Chinese magician to marry a girl from Ypps?

I asked Ernst, in my broken German, "War es nicht komisch dass ein Chinesischer Zauberer ein Yppserin heiratete?"

"YES," HE AGREED. "BUT IT WAS GREAT LOVE!!!"

ROMEO & JULIET

SAMSON & DELILAH

ANTHONY & CLEOPATRA

JOHN & YOKO

   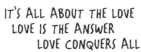

WAIT A MINUTE!
THESE ARE TRAGIC LOVE STORIES!
LET ME THINK OF SOMETHING ELSE!
...OH, IT DOESN'T MATTER...

IT'S ALL ABOUT THE LOVE
LOVE IS THE ANSWER
LOVE CONQUERS ALL
THE GREATEST GIFT IS LOVE
LOVE IS ALL YOU NEED
LOVE IS THE ONLY WAY THINGS CAN CHANGE!!

*You have no idea how many barriers that couple leaped over in cultures and bigotry to be together. And Poldi's family LOVED Sam.

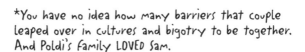

STILL, THERE WAS A SHOW TO RUN. SAM SHOWED UP LATE FOR THE WEDDING AND HAD A PERFORMANCE BOOKED THAT EVENING AND TOOK OFF RIGHT AFTER THE CEREMONY. HE WAS ON THE ROAD ALL THE TIME.

SAM IS DIRECTOR OF THE TAN KWAI TROUPE, WHO WERE KNOWN PARTICULARLY FOR THEIR HAIR TRICKS. I DON'T THINK MANY PEOPLE DID THEM AS THEY WERE EXTREMELY PAINFUL!

I WANTED TO KNOW WHAT ELSE WAS GOING ON IN THE WORLD WHILE SAM WAS DOING HIS THING. IN 1908, WHEN HE MARRIES POLDI, PU YI, THE CHILD KING, BECOMES EMPEROR OF CHINA. THE LAST EMPEROR, IT TURNS OUT, OF THE CHING DYNASTY. AND HIS FATE IS GOING TO EFFECT SAM DIRECTLY.

1908

THE LONG BRAID, OR 'KEW,' THAT SAM USED IN HIS ACT, WAS ASSOCIATED WITH THE CHING DYNASTY. IT WAS THERE SO YOU COULD EASILY BE PULLED UP TO THE HEAVENS WHEN YOU DIE.

IN 1909, MY GRANDMOTHER, MINA IS BORN.

IN 1910, HER SISTER, POLDI, IS BORN.

IN 1911...

...PU YI AND THE CHING EMPIRE ARE OVERTHROWN BY REPUBLICANS. WEARING LONG HAIR IS FORBIDDEN. THOSE WHO REFUSE TO CUT THEIR KEWS FACE EXECUTION. NO MORE HAIR... NO MORE HAIR TRICKS FOR LONG TACK SAM AND CO. EVEN THOUGH THEY ARE IN EUROPE. JUST ANOTHER EXAMPLE, I GUESS, OF HOW POLITICS AFFECTS ART!

1908
MIDDLE EAST:
Oil found in Persia

FILM:
The Adventures of Dollie,
D. W. Griffith's 1st film

ART:
CUBISM Braque and Picasso
Picasso paints
Les Desmoiselles D'Avignon

TECHNOLOGY:
Model T. 1st car
available for masses in four colors

MUSIC:
The Firebird
written by Stravinsky

1911
POPULAR SONG:
"Oh, You Beautiful Doll"

ART:
Mona Lisa stolen
from the Louvre, Paris

1912
North Pole conquered

Titantic sinks

POPULAR SONG:
"My Melancholy Baby"

ART :
The Afternoon of a Faun,
ballet collaboration between
Nijinsky, Débussy and Mallarmé

1913
POPULAR SONG:
"St. Louis Blues"

1914
WWI begins

FILM:
Caught in a Cabaret
with Charlie Chaplin

In 1914...the economy is terrible in Europe. Sam leaves his young family behind...

...and sails off to America, to New York City, by steamship. It only takes about a week.

The popular entertainment of the day –Vaudeville– is in full swing. The Tan Kwai Troupe has a full show of traditional Chinese circus acts. According to the reviews I found in *Variety* magazine, the audiences loved it... there was just one problem...

THEY GOT MISTAKEN FOR THE FAMOUS CROONER... EVA TANGUAY

SO THEY CHANGED THEIR NAME... AND GOT BOOKED AS A DOG ACT.

So, he changed their name to The Long Tack Sam Troupe.

*illustration from the Tivoli theater catalogue, New Zealand 1924.

WHAT DOES THAT NAME MEAN?

郎 SOME PEOPLE SAY THIS SOUNDS LIKE WOLF OR DRAGON BUT MEANS BRIDEGROOM OR YOUNG VENDOR

德 SOME SAY THIS SYMBOL MEANS VIRTUE

山 "SAM" IS THE ENGLISH WAY OF SAYING "SHAN", WHICH MEANS MOUNTAIN

SO, LONG TACK SAM IS A VENDOR WHO IS A MOUNTAIN OF VIRTUE" SOME PEOPLE SAY "L'UNG T'A SHAN" IS SHANGHAI-NESE FOR "TAKE IT EASY"

I KEEP ON LOOKING FOR SAM'S STORY. EVERYWHERE I GO, I FIND ANOTHER PICTURE, I GET ANOTHER TALE.

JAY MARSHALL, MAGICIAN
CHICAGO, ILLINOIS

★ BERT ALLERTON

★ LONG TACK S

★ JAY MARSHALL

SOC
Gol
AND
N
The
★ BOB PORTER
★ HARRISON, JR

I WANTED TO FIND OUT MORE ABOUT THIS STRANGE WORLD. THE MORE I KNEW, THE MORE I KNEW I DIDN'T KNOW MUCH. YOU KNOW?

I WENT BACK TO CHICAGO TO MEET UP WITH JAY MARSHALL AT HIS MAGIC SHOP IN 1999. JAY WAS THE DEAN OF THE SOCIETY OF AMERICAN MAGICIANS (S.A.M.). HE PLAYED ON A BILL WITH LONG TACK SAM WHEN HE WAS 19 YEARS OLD AND HAD SOME STORIES. HE DIDN'T EVEN KNOW THAT SAM WAS REALLY CHINESE! HE SAID A LOT OF MAGICIANS PRETENDED TO BE FROM EXOTIC PLACES. SINCE VERY FEW PEOPLE TRAVELLED AT THAT TIME, YOU COULD GET AWAY WITH IT. THE BEAUTY AND THE MYSTERY OF THE ORIENT SUITED MAGIC WELL.

MAYBE IT'S TIME FOR A LITTLE HISTORY LESSON HERE.

← amf levitating

FU - MANCHU

FU MANCHU WAS A VERY FAMOUS CHINESE PERFORMER. HIS REAL NAME WAS DAVID BAMBERG.

HE WAS THE SON OF OKITO, WHO WAS A DUTCH GUY WITH A CHINESE ACT AND A JAPANESE NAME. ➡

LONG TACK SAM KNEW AND ADMIRED THEM BOTH.

JOHN MULHOLLAND WORE MASKS. IT DIDN'T MATTER TO AUDIENCES IF PEOPLE WERE REALLY CHINESE OR NOT. AS I SAID, THE ORIENT REPRESENTED MYSTERY! IT DREW IN THE CROWDS! BUT USUALLY WESTERN IMPERSONATORS WERE MORE POPULAR THAN 'REAL' CHINESE PERFORMERS. BEFORE LONG TACK SAM, THERE WAS ONE NOTICEABLE EXCEPTION...

CHING LING FOO

(incidentally, not his real name, either!)
*pictured with Harry Kellar

Ching Ling Foo was so successful...

that one Billy Robinson copied his act... and his name.

CHUNG CHALLENGED CHING TO A DUEL TO SEE WHO WAS THE BETTER MAGICIAN. CHING NEVER SHOWED UP AND WENT BACK TO CHINA. CHUNG STAYED IN CHARACTER OFF-STAGE AND ON. HE EVEN SPOKE FAKE CHINESE TO REPORTERS. HE WAS SO CONVINCING THAT HE SUFFERED DISCRIMINATION WHEN HE TOURED CANADA.

CHUNG DIED ON STAGE, DURING HIS FAMOUS BULLET-CATCHING TRICK. (IT WAS AN ACCIDENT. GUN POWDER HAD ERODED THE CLOSED CHAMBER THAT WAS SUPPOSED TO PROTECT HIM).

AUDIENCES LIKE DAREDEVILS AND LONG TACK SAM'S ACT WAS FULL OF DISPLAYS OF ACROBATIC SKILLS WITH FIRE, TRIDENTS AND SWORDS.

I GOT A TIP FROM MARK MITTON IN NYC TO GO TO SAN FRANCISCO TO TALK TO LU YI, FORMER HEAD OF THE SHANGHAI ACROBATIC TROUPE WHO TEACHES AT THE SCHOOL FOR CIRCUS ARTS.

4

Undoubtedly, the World's Finest ORIENTAL PRESENTATION

Long Tack Sam Troupe

A Program of Incomparable Chinese Entertainment

Routines, So Unusual, So Amazing, So Thoroughly Thrilling That Space Here
Is Inadequate to Attempt a Detailed Description. Audiences All Over the
World Have Pronounced Them the Peer of All Far-East Combinations.

EVERY ACT *IN THIS CATALOG CONTROLLED EXCLUSIVELY*
BY BARNES~CARRUTHERS FAIR BOOKING ASSOCIATION, Inc.
"SERVICE and SATISFACTION"

LU YI EXPLAINED TO ME THAT LONG TACK SAM'S ACT WAS PART OF A 3,000 YEAR OLD CHINESE TRADITION. ALL PERFORMANCE ARTS- FROM OPERA TO MARTIAL ARTS- CAME FROM ACROBATS.

YOU DO MAGIC?

I MAKE FILMS.

THAT KIND OF HANDSTAND IS NAMED AFTER AN ANIMAL- "LODZ-DE"

NOW, THEY SPIN WITH WAY MORE PLATES!

LU YI SAYS HE CAN HELP ME GO TO CHINA TO DO MORE RESEARCH ON LONG TACK SAM. HE SAYS MY FAMILY IS FROM A LONG LINE OF ACROBATS AND THEY STILL LIVE THERE.

BUT FIRST, I WENT BACK TO VANCOUVER, B.C. TO VISIT THE MUSEUM OF ANTHROPOLOGY- WHERE I HEARD MY GRANDMOTHER HAD DONATED ONE OF LONG TACK SAM'S BACKDROPS... IT WAS HUGE!

MUSEUM OF ANTHROPOLOGY VANCOUVER, BRITISH COLUMBIA

30

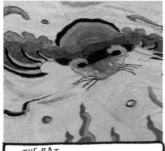

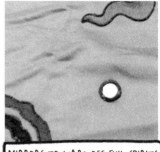

BUDDHIST SYMBOLS:

THE DRAGON...
FOR STRENGTH

THE BAT...
FOR LUCK

MIRRORS TO WARD OFF EVIL SPIRITS

I couldn't believe how opulent it was! And the colors! Made by the silk weavers of Suchow back in the 1920's. The museum had it rolled up in the back and didn't have any information about its history, except it belonged to a guy- Long Dick Shang- who knew Jack Benny.

SURE, LIFE SEEMED PRETTY GLAMOROUS FOR THE TROUPE BACK THEN...

BUT REMEMBER, SOCIALIZING AS AN ASIAN IN NORTH AMERICA THEN WAS NOT EASY!

Other Asian performers told me they had to be twice as good as a White man to succeed!

Here is a copy of an article by Bennett Cerf, that appeared in the Vidette Messenger, Valparaiso, Indiana, 1967. It'll give you an idea of how outrageous the Sinophobia (read "racism") was and how Long Tack Sam dealt with it.

*Thanks to Michael Perovich for passing this on.

TRY AND STOP ME

At the Palace Theatre, in the days when headliners fought with each other over top billing and who was going to get the best dressing rooms, Bert Fitzgibbons, famous monologist, was outraged to discover that a Chinese magician named Long Tack Sam was not only billed above him, but was carded to proceed him with his act. At the opening Monday Matinee, recalls Richard Harrity, Fitzgibbons marched on stage while

*From a 1967 illustration

Long Tack Sam was taking a bow, thrust a bunch of soiled shirts into his arms and rasped, "I want these back by Saturday night, and go easy on the starch."

Harrity neglects to provide an ending to this anecdote, but I learn from a Chinese old-timer that Long Tack Sam delivered one Oriental uppercut that caught bold "Bertie" square on the button and laid him out cold with the happy audience hollering for more.

THERE IS ABSOLUTELY <u>NO WAY</u> THIS STORY COULD HAVE ENDED AS TRIUMPHANTLY FOR MY GREAT-GRANDFATHER AS THE OLD-TIMER WOULD HAVE US BELIEVE. BUT THAT'S WHAT MYTHS ARE MADE OF! ALSO, LONG TACK SAM WAS EXTREMELY HANDSOME, (SUPER HUNK), WHICH IS <u>NOT</u> PROPERLY REPRESENTED IN THE ILLUSTRATION OF THE "BUCKTOOTHED CHINAMAN."
MAYBE THE ARTIST HAD DRAWING PROBLEMS, TOO!

It doesn't phase Sam...

He plays all over America,

From Broadway to veteran's halls...

Traveling with an international group of vaudeville performers... every little town... and picking up everybody's accents.

PEOPLE SAID HE SPOKE FRENCH... GERMAN...

... YIDDISH...

ALL WITH AN AMERICAN ACCENT. OR WAS THAT A MANDARIN ACCENT? AN ITALIAN ACCENT?

A "multilinguist"– Long Tack Sam borrows everything from everyone and incorporates it into his act...

And shapes his show–and himself– into a cosmopolitan mix of non-stop entertainment. He does comedy, he does impersonations. American audiences eat it up.

DAMN CLEVER, THESE CHINESE.

IN THE BILLY ROSE COLLECTION OF THE NEW YORK PUBLIC LIBRARY I FOUND OUT SAM SHARED THE BILL WITH THE MARX BROTHERS ON THE 2ND-EVER SHOW AT THE PALACE THEATRE, BROADWAY'S PREEMINENT VAUDEVILLE HOUSE.

HE PLAYED THERE SEVEN TIMES! THAT'S MORE THAN HARRY HOUDINI (OKAY, SO HOUDINI DIED PREMATURELY). THE POINT IS... LONG TACK SAM WAS BIG!

I go to visit my cousin, Carol (Ruby Li), in Bolinas, California. A place where they take down the road signs so no one can find it. She is a painter, and believes in spirits. There are chickens where she lives. Long Tack Sam's animal spirit is a rooster.

THIS WAY / NOT THIS WAY

WHEN INTERVIEWED FOR A NEWSPAPER IN 1915, SAM SAID THAT THE DIFFERENCE BETWEEN EAST & WEST MAGIC WAS THAT WESTERNERS PRESENTED THEMSELVES AS SKILLFUL TRICKSTERS. EASTERN MAGICIANS WERE TRUE CONJURERS AND NECROMANCERS WHO KEPT THE COMPANY OF SPIRITS.

Why Chinese Magic is the Real Thing

And American Magicians Are Self-Confessed Fakers—Although, as Long Tack Sam Admits, There is Some Merit in the Idea of a Speaking Image of Buddha Equipped With a Concealed Telephone.

BUT NO MAGIC CAN BEAT A LETTER FROM HOME. I FOUND THIS PICTURE OF SAM GETTING A MISSIVE. I IMAGINE IT'S FROM POLDI, TELLING HIM HOW HARD THINGS ARE IN EUROPE.

HOW DOES HE FIND OUT WAR BREAKS OUT IN EUROPE IN 1914?

DOES HE READ IT IN THE PAPERS? HE MUST GO CRAZY WITH WORRY.

WITH THE SINKING OF THE LUSITANIA, FOR STARTERS, NO PASSENGERSHIP WAS WILLING TO CROSS THE ATLANTIC WITH GERMAN U-BOATS LURKING BELOW. LONG TACK SAM CAN'T SEND MONEY HOME TO HIS FAMILY.

I GO TO NASHVILLE, TENNESSEE, WHERE THE EGYPTIAN HALL MUSEUM OF MAGIC WAS IN THE HOME OF DAVID & MARY JANE PRICE, PASSED ON DOWN BY HIS FATHER. IT WAS A TREASURE CHEST OF ARTIFACTS.

DAVID & MARY JANE PRICE JR.
EGYPTIAN HALL MUSEUM, 1999

In the Price library, I find another version of the history of Long Tack Sam. A very different one!

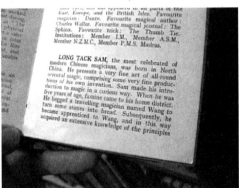

East, Europe, and the British Isles. Favourite magician: Dante. Favourite magical author: Charles Waller. Favourite magical journal: The Sphinx. Favourite trick: The Thumb Tie. Institutions: Member I.M., Member A.S.M., Member N.Z.M.C., Member P.M.S. Madras.

LONG TACK SAM, the most celebrated of modern Chinese magicians, was born in North China. He presents a very fine act of all-round oriental magic, comprising some very fine productions of his own invention. Sam made his introduction to magic in a curious way. When he was five years of age, famine came to his home district. He begged a travelling magician named Wang to turn some stones into bread. Subsequently, he became apprenticed to Wang, and in this way acquired an extensive knowledge of the principles

SURELY, YOU DON'T BELIEVE EVERYTHING YOU READ IN PRINT?

?

Curiouser and curiouser. This "finding the real story" was starting to become a little complicated. And I was working so hard! In this version, Sam has connections to the imperial court. Could it be true?

It begins in the same way, in a small village in China...

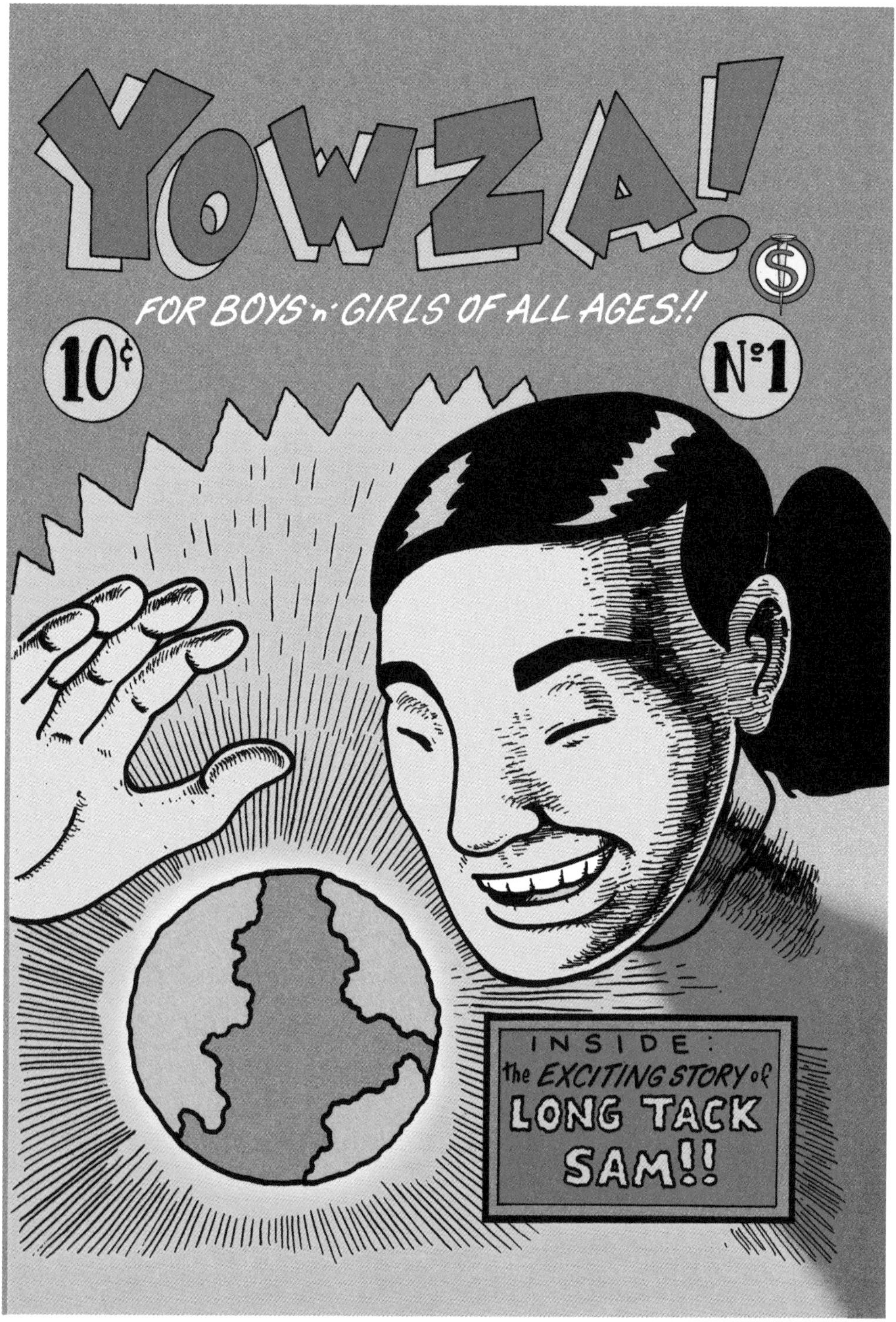
YOWZA!
FOR BOYS 'n' GIRLS OF ALL AGES!!
10¢
No 1
INSIDE:
the EXCITING STORY of
LONG TACK
SAM!!

CHINA AT THE END OF THE NINETEENTH CENTURY WAS A LAND RAVAGED BY DROUGHT, FAMINE AND REBELLION. IN A NORTHERN VILLAGE LIVED LONG TACK SAM.

HIS FATHER WAS AN IMPERIAL OFFICER IN THE SERVICE OF THE EMPEROR. LONG'S BOYHOOD WAS THAT OF THE USUAL CHINESE CHILD OF HIS STATION.

IT WOULD HAVE BEEN QUITE DIFFERENT HAD HE NOT TRIED, WITH SOME OTHER BOYS, TO SEE WHO COULD THROW A STONE HIGHEST IN THE AIR.

LONG WON, BUT HIS STONE CAME DOWN AMONG THE JADE DISPLAY OF A STREET MERCHANT AND BROKE A JADE BRACELET. THE PEDDLAR WAS FURIOUS, AND THE BOY WAS BADLY FRIGHTENED.

HE BEGAN TO RUN--

AS HE RAN HE BECAME MORE FRIGHTENED FOR HE REALIZED THAT AS AN OFFICIAL'S SON HE WOULD BE RECOGNIZED.

RATHER THAN RISK THE PARENTAL WRATH HE DECIDED THAT THE ONLY THING TO DO WAS TO LEAVE HOME FOREVER ...

AND START OUT INTO THE WORLD TO MAKE HIS FORTUNE. HE WAS NOT YET NINE YEARS OLD.

HE KEPT ON GOING UNTIL FINALLY HE CAME TO A RIVER WHERE A CROWD WHO WERE WAITING FOR A FERRY STOOD WATCHING A BOY JUGGLE.

THIS BOY WAS ONLY A LITTLE OLDER THAN LONG HIMSELF.

THE CROWD SEEMED AMUSED AND GAVE THE BOY SEVERAL COPPERS...

WHILE LONG, WHO COULD NOT ONLY THROW A STONE VERY HIGH BUT WHO COULD DO SEVERAL SIMPLE FEATS OF JUGGLING, WATCHED ENVIOUSLY.

HE FINALLY GOT UP ENOUGH COURAGE TO STEP INTO THE CIRCLE AND OFFER TO CONTINUE THE ENTERTAINMENT.

HE WAS LIKED, AND BECAUSE HE WAS SUCH A LITTLE FELLOW THEY WERE AS GENEROUS TO HIM AS THEY HAD BEEN TO THE BOY WHO WAS BETTER TRAINED.

AS LONG WAS PICKING UP THE COINS WHICH HAD BEEN THROWN TO HIM, THE FERRY CAME AND THE PEOPLE ALL GOT ON BOARD.

HEY! YOU'RE PRETTY GOOD! EVER THINK OF GOING PRO? I'M TRAINING WITH A MAGICIAN IN TIENTSIN.

LONG LIKED THE IDEA OF BEING A MAGICIAN'S ASSISTANT AND ASKED THE BOY IF HE COULD GO WITH HIM. THE BOY NOT ONLY AGREED TO THAT, BUT ASSURED LONG THAT THE MASTER MAGICIAN WOULD BE GLAD TO HAVE ANOTHER APPRENTICE.

THE TWO BOYS PERFORMED THEIR JUGGLING FEATS WHENEVER THEY GOT HUNGRY AND WERE USUALLY FORTUNATE ENOUGH TO FIND PEOPLE WHO WERE SUFFICIENTLY AMUSED TO GIVE MONEY OR FOOD.

THEY TRAMPED DAY AFTER DAY UNTIL THEY MADE FRIENDS WITH A RIVER BOATMAN WITH WHOM THEY RODE THE REST OF THE WAY.

THAT IS, THEY RODE DURING THE TIME THAT THE WIND BLEW. WHEN THE WIND GAVE OUT THEY WOULD ALL TAKE HOLD OF A ROPE AND WALK ALONG THE RIVER BANK PULLING THE BOAT.

THEY ARRIVED AT TIENTSIN EARLY ONE MORNING. LONG WAS TOLD BY THE OLDER BOY TO STAND OUTSIDE THE CITY WALL AND WAIT UNTIL HE WENT TO HIS MASTER--

-- BUT HE DID NOT RETURN.

A TIRED AND HUNGRY LONG TACK SAM WALKED AROUND UNTIL HE FOUND THE FAIRGROUNDS.

HE PASSED THE STORY-TELLER, THE MAN WHO MADE SHADOW PICTURES AND THE FORTUNE-TELLER.

FINALLY HE CAME TO A LARGE CIRCLE OF PEOPLE WHO WERE LAUGHING AND APPLAUDING, BUT THEY WERE STANDING SO CLOSE TOGETHER HE COULDN'T SEE WHAT THE PERFORMER WAS DOING.

HE WRIGGLED HIS WAY INTO THE CENTER OF THE CIRCLE JUST IN TIME TO SEE THE LAST TRICK OF THE MAGICIAN WHO WAS CREATING SUCH MERRIMENT

LONG KNEW HE HAD FOUND HIS FUTURE MASTER!

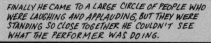

NOW, YOU HAVE TO ADMIT, THAT'S A PRETTY GOOD STORY!

*but I still wanted to find out about the man, not just the myth

SAM MAY BE ABLE TO CHANGE HIS OWN HISTORY, BUT HE CAN'T CHANGE THE WORLD'S. EUROPE IS STILL BURNING,

AND THE WAR IS NOT OVER UNTIL 1918, WHEN GERMANY AND AUSTRIA CONCEDE DEFEAT ON VERY HARSH TERMS, INDEED.

1915

POPULAR SONG:
"Keep the Home Fires Burning"

FILM:
Birth of a Nation,
D. W. Griffiths

ART:
Piet Mondrian paints
Pier and Ocean

LITERATURE:
Kafka writes *The Metamorphosis*

1917

CANADA
Women get the vote

U.S.A.
Joins war against Germany

BRITAIN
Promises Jewish homeland to convince Jews to join Allied war effort

FRANCE
Mata Hari executed in Paris

RUSSIA
Revolution—Lenin and the Bolsheviks seize power

POPULAR SONG:
"Over There!"

FILM:
The Poor Little Rich Girl
with Mary Pickford

1918

U.S.A.
Women get the vote

POPULAR SONG:
"You're a Grand Ol' Flag"

1919

I can't imagine what it must have been like for Sam, after his big success in the U.S., To come back to Europe.

He's finally reunited with the love of his life, Poldi and his girls. But Austria is impoverished and destroyed by war.

HERE'S WHAT I THINK HE DID. A) THE MOST IMPORTANT THING WAS TO KEEP THE FAMILY TOGETHER.
B) SO HE MAKES POLDI HIS ASSISTANT AND GETS HIS KIDS IN THE SHOW.

SIMPLE, RIGHT?

Poldi had never been outside of Austria before...

...And theirs was to be a life of non-stop world travel...

I WAS CERTAINLY BEGINNING TO UNDERSTAND THE DIFFICULTY OF THAT!

AND IT WAS THE WORLD OF THE CIRCUS... LIONS, TIGERS, ELEPHANTS, COWGIRLS AND INDIANS...

POLDI TOOK TO IT, THOUGH, AND WITH HER THRIFTY MANAGEMENT, SAM STARTED TO SAVE SOME OF THAT MONEY HE'D BEEN MAKING.

45

MAYBE YOU'RE WONDERING WHY I KEPT ON TRAVELING, TRYING TO FIND A MAN I NEVER KNEW. I DID NOT KNOW. IF SOMEONE GAVE ME A CLUE, AN OPPORTUNITY TO MEET SOMEONE, I SAID YES.

← Stickgirl always says "yes"

ELAINE LUND
AMERICAN MUSEUM OF MAGIC

I went to Marshall, Michigan, to meet Elaine Lund, who looks after her late husband Robert's collection of magic memorabelia, known as the "American Museum of Magic."

She told me about lots of tricks magicians would pull to try and get their gear across the country. Sometimes 5 tons of gear and more!

ELAINE AND ROBERT NEVER HAD A PROPER HONEYMOON AND EVERY WEEKEND WAS SPENT SORTING THROUGH MAGIC ARCANA, AS A HOBBY. LOOKS LIKE I WASN'T THE ONLY PERSON WHO GETS OBSESSED ABOUT THINGS.

Here are some pictures with Sam and Poldi on the road. Remember, they've got their little girls, too.

These photographs come from one of my great-grandmother's albums, circa 1915-1918. I think that's Stan Laurel in the bottom left picture.

Everyone on the road has to work, so it's not long before Sam's daughters, Mina and Poldi, are incorporated into the act.

THEY WERE GIVEN THE MORE CHINESEY SOUNDING STAGE NAMES OF MI-NA AND NEE-SA. THEY WERE BILLED AS TWINS, TOO. THEY DANCED AND SANG AND PLAYED INSTRUMENTS. SOUNDS LIKE FUN, BUT IT WAS HARD WORK! THEIR CHILDHOOD WAS OFFICIALLY OVER.

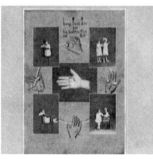

These girls were actually competing for audiences with Harry Houdini... the great escape artist and illusionist, who, by the way...

Invited Sam to be part of his Elite Magicians' Club, and then patented one of Sam's staple acts... the Needle Swallowing Trick... and wouldn't let anyone perform it. Since it was from an ancient Chinese tradition, this wasn't really legal... but Houdini had so much clout, he made it happen.

Here's a picture of Sam and Poldi doing the trick.

REVOLUTIONS, RACISM, RIVAL MAGICIANS...
LONG TACK SAM ADJUSTS.
THAT'S SHOW BUSINESS.

1920

POPULAR SONG:
"When My Baby Smiles At Me"

FILM:
Sex, with Harold Lloyd

ART:
DADAISM Marcel Duchamp's "Urinal"

SPORTS:
Babe Ruth (24 yrs old) signs to NewYork Yankees for $100,000.

IRELAND
Dublin, Bloody Sunday—IRA kill 14 British officers.
Black and Tans take retribution out on civilians

1921

FILM:
The Kid, with Jackie Coogan and Charlie Chaplin.

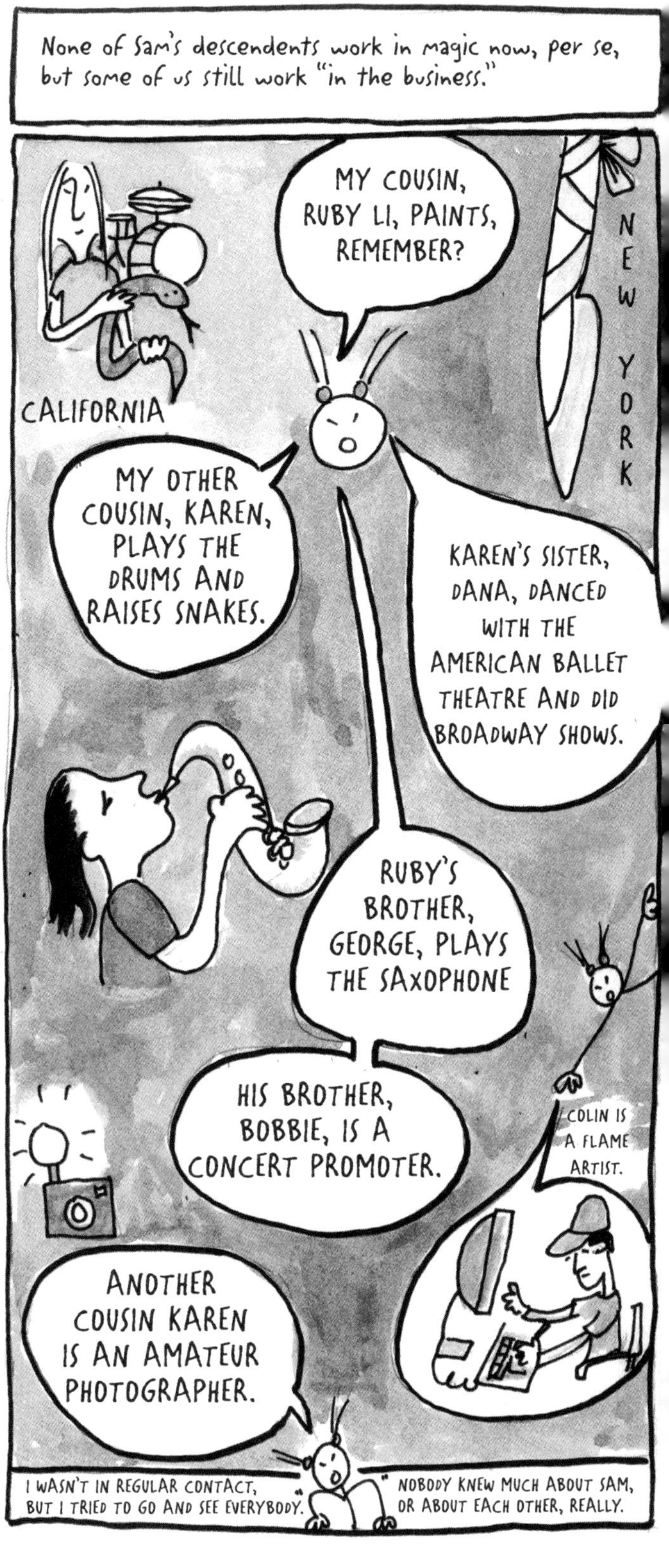
None of Sam's descendents work in magic now, per se, but some of us still work "in the business."
CALIFORNIA
MY COUSIN, RUBY LI, PAINTS, REMEMBER?
NEW YORK
MY OTHER COUSIN, KAREN, PLAYS THE DRUMS AND RAISES SNAKES.
KAREN'S SISTER, DANA, DANCED WITH THE AMERICAN BALLET THEATRE AND DID BROADWAY SHOWS.
RUBY'S BROTHER, GEORGE, PLAYS THE SAXOPHONE
HIS BROTHER, BOBBIE, IS A CONCERT PROMOTER.
COLIN IS A FLAME ARTIST.
ANOTHER COUSIN KAREN IS AN AMATEUR PHOTOGRAPHER.
I WASN'T IN REGULAR CONTACT, BUT I TRIED TO GO AND SEE EVERYBODY."
"NOBODY KNEW MUCH ABOUT SAM, OR ABOUT EACH OTHER, REALLY.

In its heyday, vaudeville was _huge_!! At the Hippodrome in NYC, over one thousand performers shared a revolving stage over a block long. Long Tack Sam was having a ball. (Cary Grant—then the unicycle—riding Archibald Leach—would have shared the stage in 1922.)

I found some letters Long Tack Sam wrote to his friend, William Goldston, in England, about his time in New York City in 1922. (Goldston built magic tricks.)

Dear friend Goldston,

Lester arrived on Wednesday. I had to rush to the Hippodrome for the matinee. I am doing very nicely. Will stay in New York the full season. I am giving all the publicity I can about you to the magicians over here (Don't tell Clayton! Ha! Ha!) Maurice is going good on the Pantages tour.* Gus Fowler is a sensation on the Keith tour. Giska and several other magicians are in my apartment every evening.

*A 'tour' is a theatrical circuit

*filming of The Sheik, 1921

*audiences still liked to see exotic lands

BUT THINGS WERE CHANGING FOR VAUDEVILLE IN AMERICA. MOVING PICTURES STARTED TO BE INCORPORATED BETWEEN LIVE ACTS... THEY TURNED OUT TO BE CHEAPER TO RUN AND COULD RUN ALL DAY...

*LAUREL & HARDY IMPERSONATORS

VAUDEVILLIANS START TO COMPETE WITH MOVIE STARS.

STAGE CREWS ARE BEING UNIONIZED. ACTS ARE GETTING SMALLER. PEOPLE PERFORMED IN FRONT OF THE CURTAIN, BECAUSE YOU DIDN'T HAVE TO PAY UNION DUES OVER THE ORCHESTRA PIT!

FAIR WAGES

ISN'T THAT RUDOLPH VALENTINO!?

MARY PICKFORD AMERICA'S SWEETHEART

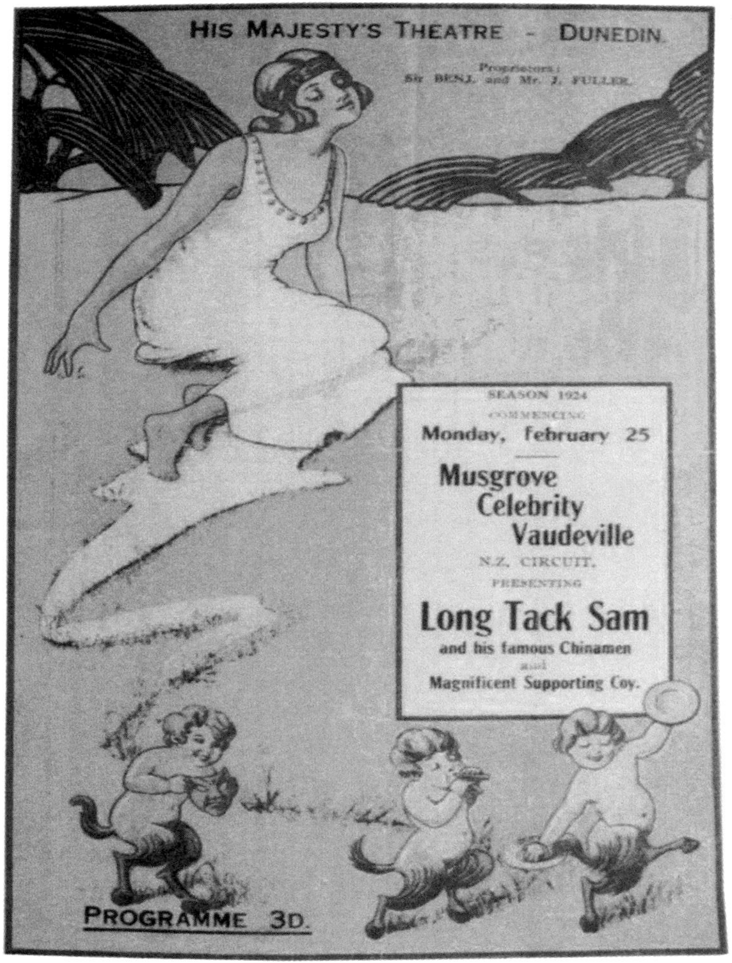
HIS MAJESTY'S THEATRE - DUNEDIN.
Proprietors: Sir BENJ. and Mr. J. FULLER.
SEASON 1924
COMMENCING
Monday, February 25
Musgrove
Celebrity
Vaudeville
N.Z. CIRCUIT.
PRESENTING
Long Tack Sam
and his famous Chinamen
and
Magnificent Supporting Coy.
PROGRAMME 3D.

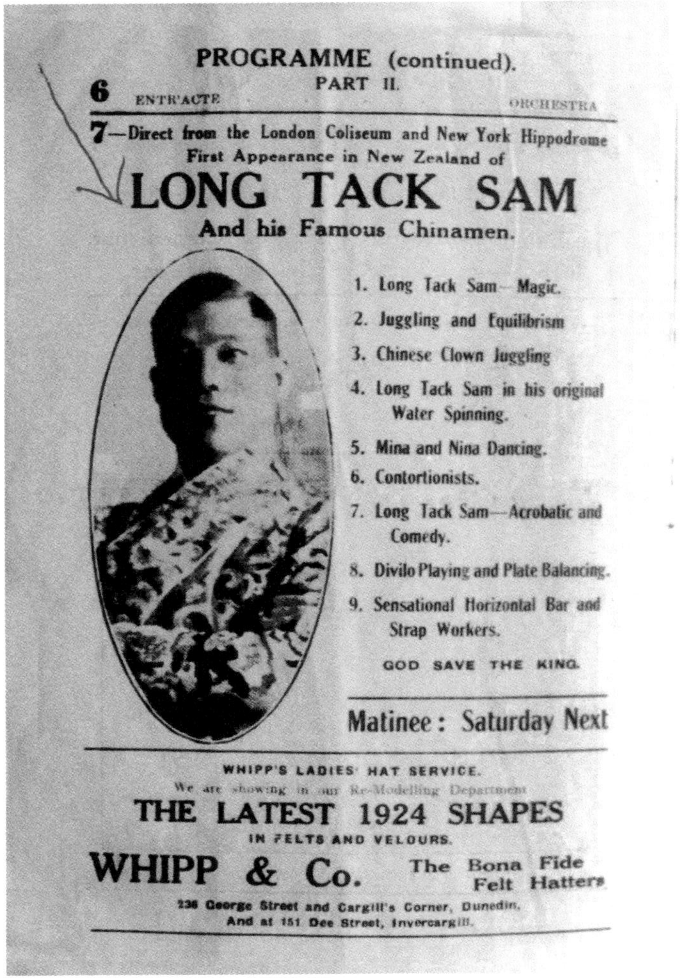
PROGRAMME (continued).
PART II.
6 ENTR'ACTE ORCHESTRA
7—Direct from the London Coliseum and New York Hippodrome
First Appearance in New Zealand of
LONG TACK SAM
And his Famous Chinamen.
1. Long Tack Sam—Magic.
2. Juggling and Equilibrism
3. Chinese Clown Juggling
4. Long Tack Sam in his original Water Spinning.
5. Mina and Nina Dancing.
6. Contortionists.
7. Long Tack Sam—Acrobatic and Comedy.
8. Divilo Playing and Plate Balancing.
9. Sensational Horizontal Bar and Strap Workers.
GOD SAVE THE KING.
Matinee: Saturday Next
WHIPP'S LADIES' HAT SERVICE.
We are showing in our Re-Modelling Department
THE LATEST 1924 SHAPES
IN FELTS AND VELOURS.
WHIPP & Co.
The Bona Fide Felt Hatters
236 George Street and Cargill's Corner, Dunedin,
And at 151 Dee Street, Invercargill.

IT'S TIME FOR THE LONG TACK SAM TROUPE TO LEAVE AMERICA FOR OTHER, CHEAPER, SHORES. THEY CROSS THE PACIFIC, HEADING TO AUSTRALIA, NEW ZEALAND—CHINA. LOOKING FOR NEW AUDIENCES, WHERE A VAUDEVILLE SHOW COULD STILL SELL OUT A THEATRE ALL BY ITSELF.

PRINCE OF WALES THEATRE
AUCKLAND, NEW ZEALAND

SAM SAID AUSTRALIAN AND NEW ZEALAND AUDIENCES WERE THE MOST CRITICAL. OH, THEY WERE CRITICAL, ALL RIGHT...

MY BROTHER LIVES IN AUSTRALIA (HE BECAME A CITIZEN). I'VE NEVER MET MY NIECE, HIS DAUGHTER, AND MY COUSIN IS GETTING MARRIED ON A CATTLE RANCH OUTSIDE OF SYDNEY. SO, I BUY A TICKET AND FIND MYSELF DRIVING THROUGH BUSHFIRES AND BLACKFLIES AND DOING SOME RESEARCH DOWN UNDER, IN MY FATHER'S COUNTRY.

THE NEW SOUTH WALES LIBRARY IS FULL OF LONG TACK SAM MEMORABALIA

BONDI BEACH, SYDNEY

December in Sydney is sweltering. Sam was here at Christmas, too. He promoted his show by skydiving into Bondi Beach, dropping leaflets offering free tickets to that evening's performance.

Christmas Greetings and all good Wishes for your Happiness in the New Year
Mr. and Mrs. Long Tack Sam

SAM WAS WILDLY POPULAR IN AUSTRALIA. SO POPULAR PEOPLE THOUGHT HE WAS AUSTRALIAN.

NOT EVERYONE HAD THE SAME EXPERIENCE

WHEN SUN TAI WENT TO AUSTRALIA, THEY THREW HIM IN JAIL, EVEN THOUGH HE HAD BEEN INVITED! THE CHINESE COMMUNITY HAD TO GET HIM OUT

HE HAD BEEN RECCOMMENDED BY CHARLIE CHAPLIN!

SUN TAI, acrobat, Shanghai

THE ARTICLES I FOUND IN AUSTRALIA (AND EVERYWHERE, FOR THAT MATTER) TALKED ABOUT SAM'S SUCCESSES, NOT HIS PROBLEMS. HE WENT BACK EVERY YEAR. BUT I KNEW IT MUST HAVE BEEN HARD.

EVEN SPEAKING TO LIVING PEOPLE, LIKE SUN TAI, WHO HAD GONE THROUGH THE SAME ORDEALS... NO ONE REALLY WANTED TO TALK ABOUT IT... AT FIRST. YOU WOULD REALLY HAVE TO ASK THE RIGHT QUESTION.

I WONDER WHAT IT MUST HAVE BEEN LIKE WHEN SAM RETURNED TO CHINA? WHAT KIND OF ANTICIPATION AT HIS HOMECOMING?

Sam, on an ocean liner, to China, circa 1920

AMF with short, blonde hair, circa 1999.

I WANTED TO GO TO CHINA, TOO. LU YI, THE ACROBAT I MET IN SAN FRANCISCO, SAID HE'D ARRANGE THINGS FOR ME...

BUT I DON'T SPEAK CHINESE!

THAT'S OKAY, I CAN HELP.

BUT I DYED MY HAIR BLONDE!

THAT'S OKAY, TOO. CHINA IS A MODERN* COUNTRY.

Lu Yi, ACROBAT

*WELL, IT IS AND IT ISN'T. WHEN LU YI WAS HEAD OF THE SHANGHAI ACROBATIC TROUPE, THEY TOURED THE U.S. AND ONE OF HIS PERFORMERS DEFECTED (THIS WAS BEFORE CHINESE COULD EMIGRATE FROM THEIR COUNTRY). LU YI WAS HELD RESPONSIBLE WHEN HE RETURNED HOME. LATER, HE WAS ALLOWED TO MOVE TO THE STATES.

SHANG-

HAI 1920

Sam returns to China as much as a tourist as a performer... with a foreign wife. And this is the first time Poldi has experienced the culture she married into as something besides an exotic stage act. I can only imagine how much of a culture shock it would have been for her. But in some ways, show business is the same all over the world.

Something of interest: in China they have cameras on the bottom of planes...

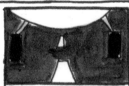

...so you can watch yourself flying and landing.

INTERESTING

BUT TERRIFYING

Shanghai, in 1999, is a modern city. In fact, it is a <u>FUTURISTIC</u> city, engulfed in the smog of history (I was there in 1988, before "economic development", and everything was completely new!! Every year it changes, faster than you can think, even...)

SHANGHAI, CHINA
1999

But Old Shanghai is still there, too... I stay at the Jin Jiang Hotel. Old time host to presidents and other luminaries. The furniture is still the same. It's a strange feeling, being there.

My great-grandparents could have sat in these chairs. It's like time stood still.

I REALLY AM BLONDE NOW

LITERALLY, RIGHT OUTSIDE THE HOTEL, IS MR. SUN TAI, THE PERSON I'VE COME TO MEET. THE ONCE WORLD-FAMOUS AWARD-WINNING MOUTH ARTIST. HE MAKES THE SOUNDS OF RIVERS AND STONES AND THUNDER. HE MET LONG TACK SAM WHEN HE FIRST CAME BACK TO CHINA. SUN TAI WAS 92 IN '99.

HOTEL

SUN TAI AND I GET IN A CAB. I HAVE NO IDEA WHERE WE ARE GOING.

Down the street is the beautiful Majestic Theatre, known as the Meigi.

AT THE HEIGHT OF HIS FAME AND FORTUNE LONG TACK SAM OWNED FIVE THEATRES IN CHINA. THEY WERE LATER TAKEN OVER BY THE COMMUNISTS.

Many of them still exist, as protected heritage buildings in the crazy, modern Shanghai. They show live performances and films!

NANKING THEATRE, 1920'S

NANKING THEATRE, 1999

AGAIN, I HAD NO IDEA THESE THEATRES EVEN EXISTED. IT WAS AMAZING!

Most of the theatre managers didn't know much about pre-WWII history of the buildings (in fact, no one was interested in history much, at all). Sun Tai was a treasure chest of knowledge.

SUN TAI HISTORY LESSON

Sun Tai told me such a lot about his time. Like I said, he didn't want to say anything negative. He toured the world as a champion mouth artist, winning international awards that he now stores underneath his bed. During the Cultural Revolution he and other acrobats were not allowed to practice their craft.

SUN TAI, mouth artist

SHANGHAI, 1920

BUT BACK TO LONG TACK SAM. SAM BRINGS WESTERN GLAMOR BACK TO THE ORIENT. IT COSTS UP TO 3 SILVER DOLLARS TO SEE A SHOW. THE SAME AS FOR A 20 LB BAG OF RICE. THE HOUSE WAS FULL EVERY NIGHT.

SAM BUILDS A HOUSE IN SHANGHAI, FOR HIS FAMILY. BUT THEN.... THEN THE STORY GETS COMPLICATED!

1ˢᵗ BMW IN SHANGHAI
*Sam was a big car fan. I think this one caught on fire!

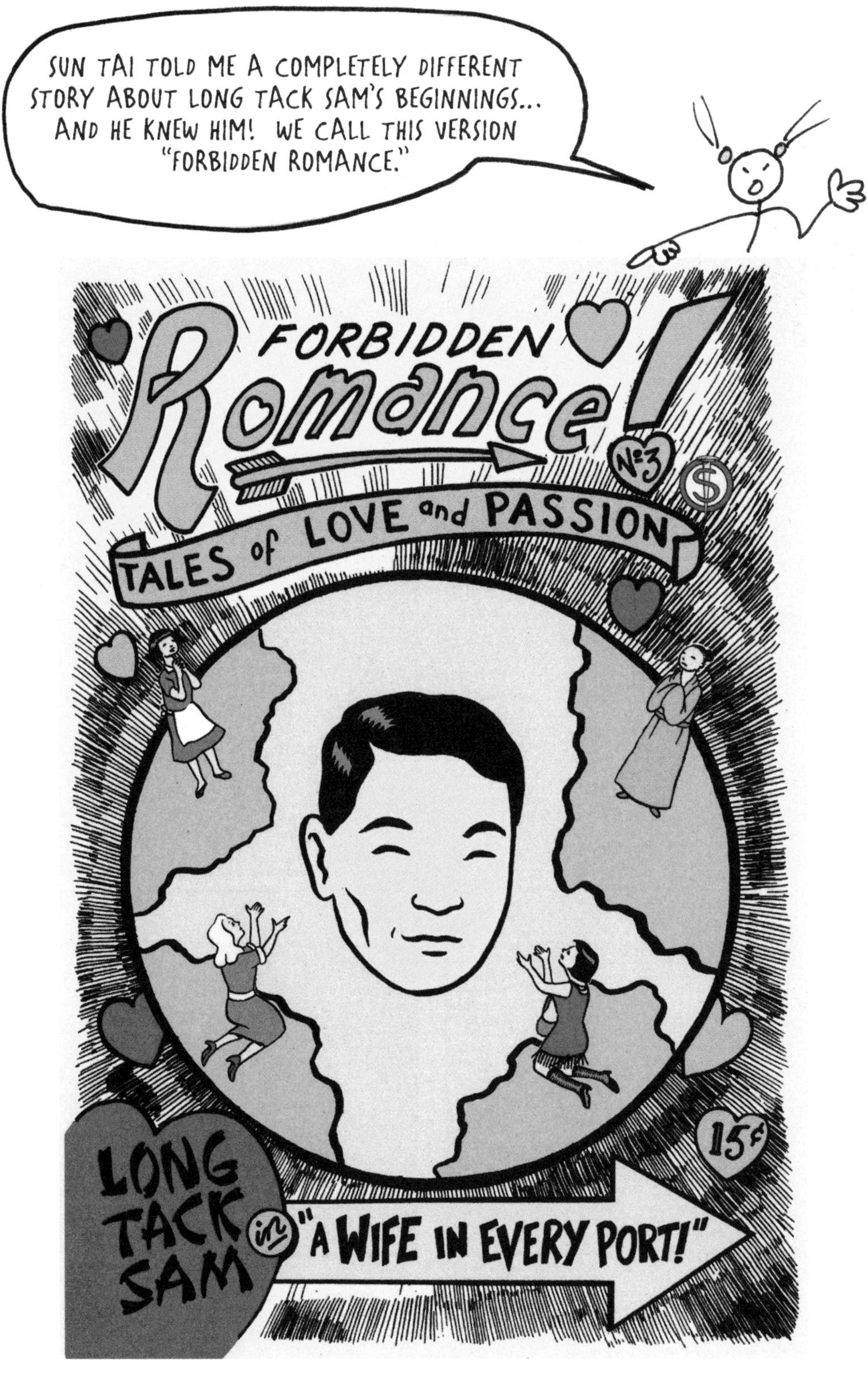
SUN TAI TOLD ME A COMPLETELY DIFFERENT STORY ABOUT LONG TACK SAM'S BEGINNINGS... AND HE KNEW HIM! WE CALL THIS VERSION "FORBIDDEN ROMANCE."
FORBIDDEN
Romance!
No3
TALES of LOVE and PASSION
15¢
LONG TACK SAM
in
"A WIFE IN EVERY PORT!"

AT THE END OF THE NINETEENTH CENTURY, CHINA WAS RAVAGED BY FAMINES, DROUGHTS AND REBELLIONS. IN THE NORTHERN VILLAGE OF WUQIAO--

--LIVED LONG TACK SAM WHO ENDURED MANY HOURS OF ACROBATICS TRAINING--

--UNDER THE GUIDANCE OF HIS OLDER BROTHER.

THE FAMOUS PERFORMER JULIAN KWAI INVITED LONG TO JOIN HIS TROUPE IN AMERICA.

AT THE AGE OF SIXTEEN LONG BECAME FAMOUS FOR HIS HANGING-BY-THE-BRAID ACT.

FUTURE SITE OF TIMES SQUARE

FOR RENT

CHEAP

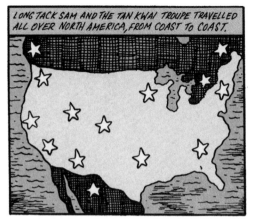

LONG TACK SAM AND THE TAN KWAI TROUPE TRAVELLED ALL OVER NORTH AMERICA, FROM COAST TO COAST.

A SWISS GIRL CAME TO THE U.S. JUST TO SEE HIM PERFORM. THEY FELL IN LOVE AND WERE MARRIED.

"Have some water."

REALLY? THE BIT ABOUT JULIAN KWAI MADE SENSE. SAM HAD BEEN WITH THE <u>TAN KWAI</u> TROUPE. BUT I HAD NEVER HEARD OF AN OLDER BROTHER OR A SWISS WIFE WHO CAME TO AMERICA TO MARRY HIM! I'M CONFUSED AND TIRED AND HAVE A BAD STOMACH.

WHAT IF THIS WAS ONLY ONE MORE STORY? SUN TAI WAS VERY YOUNG WHEN HE MET LONG TACK SAM, WHO WAS VERY FAMOUS. MAYBE IT WAS ALL RUMORS. MAYBE IT WAS LIKE MEETING MADONNA.

What I knew was that Sam came back to China with my great-grandmother, <u>Poldi</u>, who was his only wife that I had ever heard of... Poldi, who was now pregnant with her third child, 15 years after her last...

HIS BROTHER'S NAME WAS L'UNG TE SHAN.

WHAT!?

If his brother was the real Long Tack Sam, then who is my great-grandfather? What is his real name?

"I don't know. Maybe 'Shi'"

FUTURE SITE OF TIMES SQUARE

FOR RENT

CHEAP

S H ? I

So, in China, Long Tack Sam is reunited with the brother no one knew he had. The one who taught him acrobatics. The one whose name he stole. AND they fought over Poldi.

Sam's brother was either:

A) wildly jealous, and wanted to kill his brother to win his wife

B) upset Sam married a foreigner and wanted to kill HER.

(Stories diverge here)

WHATEVER THE CASE, LONG TACK SAM CREATES A NEW STORY ABOUT HIS BEGINNINGS—TOLD TO A NEW PERSON—INCORPORATING HIS NEW-FOUND FEELINGS FOR HIS LONG-LOST BROTHER.

1923

GERMANY
Mark collapses, a loaf of bread costs 200 billion DM

JAPAN
Earthquake destroys Tokyo

POPULAR SONG:
"Yes, We Have No Bananas"

FILM:
The Ten Commandments

The Hunchback of Notre Dame

AMF with brown hair

I got THIS story from N.W.Yao, LTS's son-in-law's brother, who lives in California now, but sold him that BMW in Shanghai that caught on fire. He said he'd heard this from the horse's mouth...

AT THE END OF THE NINETEENTH CENTURY CHINA WAS RAVAGED BY DROUGHT, FAMINE AND WIDESPREAD REBELLION.

IN A SMALL NORTHERN VILLAGE LIVED SAD LITTLE LONGTACK SAM WHO WAS TRAINED IN ACROBATICS BY HIS CRUEL OLDER BROTHER

OH PLEASE NUMBER ONE!! I AM TIRED AND NEED TO REST NOW!

GASP

AIE!

WHIP!

YOU WILL REST WHEN I TELL YOU TO!

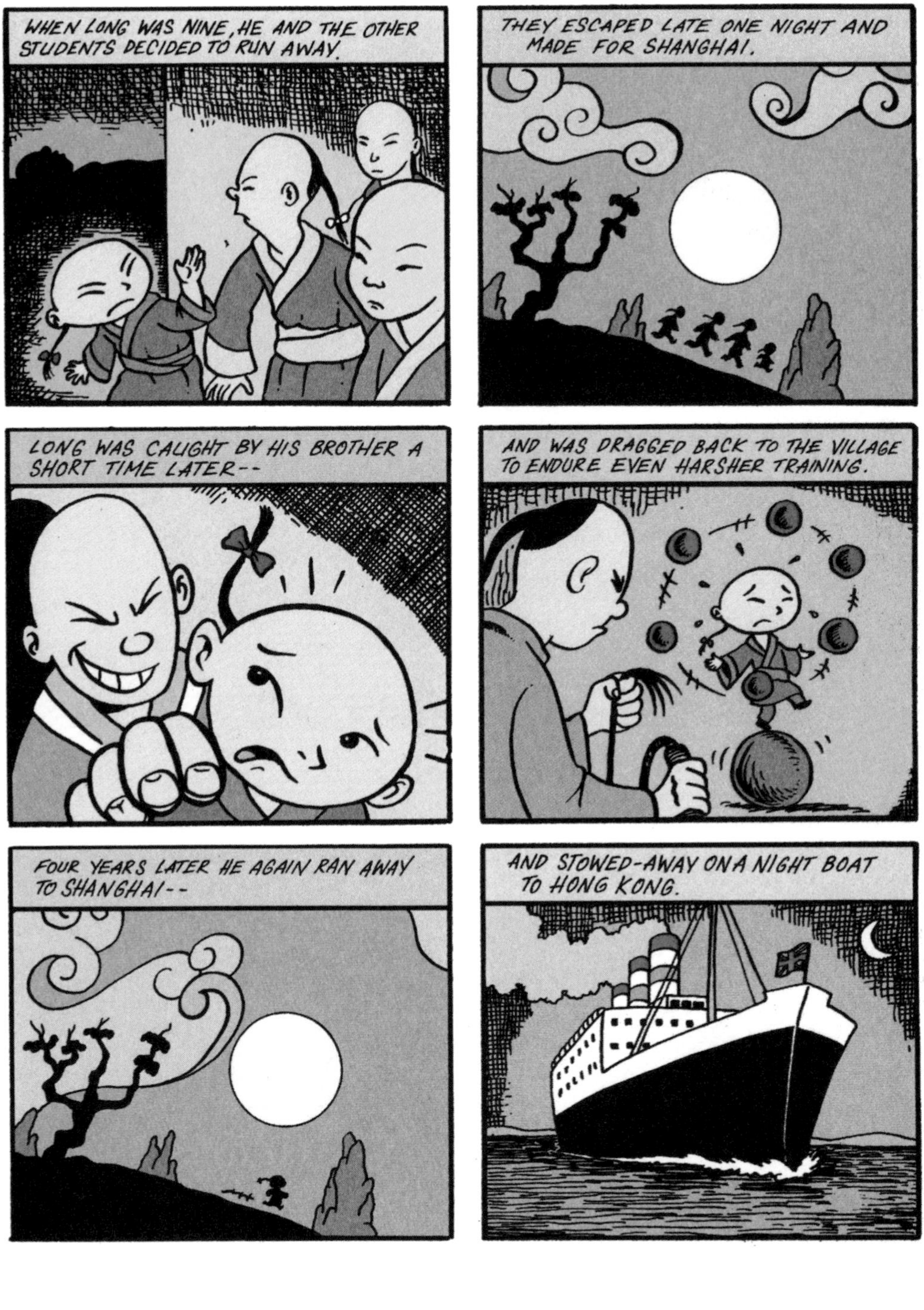
WHEN LONG WAS NINE, HE AND THE OTHER STUDENTS DECIDED TO RUN AWAY.
THEY ESCAPED LATE ONE NIGHT AND MADE FOR SHANGHAI.
LONG WAS CAUGHT BY HIS BROTHER A SHORT TIME LATER--
AND WAS DRAGGED BACK TO THE VILLAGE TO ENDURE EVEN HARSHER TRAINING.
FOUR YEARS LATER HE AGAIN RAN AWAY TO SHANGHAI--
AND STOWED-AWAY ON A NIGHT BOAT TO HONG KONG.

I WANTED TO FIND THIS BROTHER, OR AT LEAST, HIS DESCENDENTS.

BUT HOW TO FIND THEM?

WUQIAO INTERNATIONAL ACROBATIC FESTIVAL SHIJIAZHUANG, CHINA

I got on a bus to Shijiazhuang City, home of the Wuqiao Acrobatic Festival. Mr. Lu Yi had arranged an invitation for me. The name of the town my great grandfather was from! The home of Chinese acrobatics!

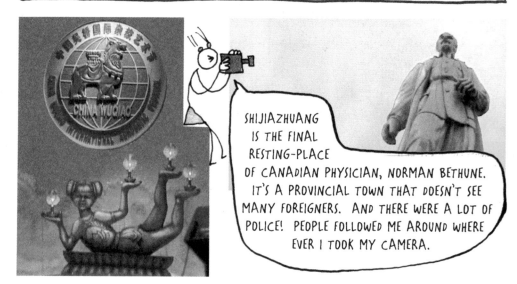

SHIJIAZHUANG IS THE FINAL RESTING-PLACE OF CANADIAN PHYSICIAN, NORMAN BETHUNE. IT'S A PROVINCIAL TOWN THAT DOESN'T SEE MANY FOREIGNERS. AND THERE WERE A LOT OF POLICE! PEOPLE FOLLOWED ME AROUND WHERE EVER I TOOK MY CAMERA.

This was an international competition for acrobats—from Sweden, Kazakhstan, China, Canada. There was no one there representing the U.S. this year, but they still had a sign.

IN CHINA, AT LEAST IN THIS PART OF CHINA, THERE IS MAGIC EVERYWHERE

Tabletop acrobatics at a restaurant

Heads of China's acrobatic troupes and me.

Our waitress does a disappearing trick

Crowds await performances at the Wuqiao International Acrobatic Festival

Videographer and police

Pretty girls wonder what to do

Diorama of ancient acrobatic tricks in a Ching Dynasty village

Russian Snake Twirler

We got to the Wuqiao Museum of Acrobatics where I see cock-fights, trained mice and magic tricks

The history of Chinese acrobatics <u>does</u> start in Shandong Province. And most acrobats were poor, and would busk on the roadsides for pennies from travelers who were entering the towns. Few toured. Even fewer toured abroad. But things change. The borders change, even. I met some acrobats who arranged to take me to the actual city of Wuqiao. Sun Tai had told me that Long Tack Sam's family were Wuqiao people.

LIANG NA, TRANSLATOR

I COULDN'T DO IT WIHOUT MY TRANSLATOR, LIANG-NA (NANCY, IN ENGLISH)

With a few phone calls, we are able to locate the exact position of Long Tack Sam's native village. This is so easy! Everyone is very excited to help me find my family.

We start off at dawn...

Liang-Na is very tired

China is mainly coal-powered, making for beautiful sunrises and dirty noses (Wuqiao is a very long way, along some very bad roads)

WUQIAO USED TO BE IN SHANDONG PROVINCE, BUT NOW IS IN HEBEI PROVINCE, BECAUSE THE BORDERS WERE MOVED. THERE IS AN ACROBATIC ACADEMY RIGHT ON THE BORDER THAT WE ARE GOING TO VISIT. THE VILLAGE LONG TACK SAM IS FROM IS JUST ON THE OTHER SIDE OF THE BORDER. THERE IS A TAXI WAITING TO TAKE ME THERE. BUT FIRST, I NEED A TOUR OF THE ACADEMY...

bus

lunch

buffalo

kids

toilet

tractor

WUQIAO ACROBATIC SCHOOL
WUQIAO, CHINA

Old-Time Magic

Waiting for the show

HERE, I BEGIN TO UNDERSTAND THE ENORMOUS TREK LONG TACK SAM MADE FROM A CHILD IN THE COUNTRY TO INTERNATIONAL CELEBRITY.

PLATE SPINNING

TUMBLING

WHAT BEGAN ON THE STREETS OF WUQIAO IS NOW INSTITUTIONALIZED ACROSS CHINA. EVERY PROVINCE HAS ITS OWN ACROBATIC SCHOOL. SELECTED CHILDREN START GOING THERE AS SOON AS THEY CAN WALK. THEY ARE TRAINED TO BE ENTERTAINERS AND THEIR WORKING LIFESPAN IS EXTREMELY SHORT.

The international community comes and chooses who they want to work with for one or two years, which is as long as the visas extend for (I think this is changing... people can actually emigrate now). Everyone—Russian circuses, Cirque du Soleil—takes young acrobats, develop routines for them, and send them back to China to train the next generation.

I go outside to get in the taxi. Finally, I will see the village of my ancestors! Meet my long lost family! But I am not allowed to go...

FALUN GONG– originally developed as a breathing exercise regime to promote good health, the enormous popularity of Falun Gong and the elevation of its leader made the Chinese government suspicious of the movement.

A Canadian journalist I meet tells me that the Falun Gong trials are happening here, and security, particularly for foreigners, is especially tight. There is no international coverage of the acrobatic competition allowed, even. I see the images on t.v. of the accused people, but I can't understand the charges, or what is going on.

I've traveled halfway around the world to get here, and they tell me to "come back next year."

I go back to my hotel room and am deathly ill. Something I ate, perhaps?

Doctors are summoned who want to put me in the hospital on an I.V. drip for several days. My translator starts to cry.

Luckily, an all-girl Swedish balancing act has an accident, and the doctors have to rush off to help, leaving me by myself to recover.

THIS IS HARDER THAN I THOUGHT IT WOULD BE.

MY VISA EXPIRES SOON AND IT IS TIME TO LEAVE CHINA.

I HAVE THIS SAME PROBLEM WITH BORDERS ALL OVER THE WORLD.

WAAH!

Shades of when I was born!

On a train, crossing between Switzerland and Italy... passport check.

I can only _imagine_ the hassles Sam encountered traveling around the world with his troupe of Chinese acrobats! His transcontinental schedule was tight and often required last-minute shipboardings, customs clearances and border crossings.

How did he deal with the RED TAPE?

Dad   Mum

I GO TO VISIT MY PARENTS, WHO NOW LIVE IN ENGLAND(!) MY MOTHER HOLDS A BRITISH PASSPORT. MY FATHER HAS TO APPLY FOR ONE. IT TAKES YEARS. I CAN'T EVEN GET A WORKING VISA...

The don't know much about Long Tack Sam's peregrinations—in fact, at this point in my search, they are not very curious—"Why do I care?"— but my uncle has an interesting story.

Solar 1
*human-powered, solar-
paneled aircraft 1979

My mom's brother, Fred, is an architect and inventor and jazz pianist. He used to build human-powered aircraft, and is afraid of flying! He overcame his fears and got his glider's license a few years ago. "Now, I don't know where I heard this from, but I'm sure it's true..."

RUSSIA

WHERE'S YOUR VISA?

VISA?

"Sam had to do a border crossing... I think it was Russia. But they stopped him and asked for his visa. But he didn't have a visa..."

WORLD TOUR

LAP SANG SU CHONG

CHINESE TEA

"So, he went to the back, somewhere..."

"...found a box of Chinese tea..."

"...cut out the label..."

"...some little red label with Chinese writing..."

"...presented it to the border guard and he got through! And that was his visa."

THAT DOESN'T HAPPEN ANYMORE!

LONDON, ENGLAND

I WENT TO LONDON, TO THE EXCLUSIVE MAGICIAN'S CLUB, THE MAGIC CIRCLE. MAGIC IS A STRANGE WORLD, AND THIS IS ITS MOST SECRET OF SOCIETIES. STILL, PEOPLE HAVE BEEN WILLING TO HELP ME DO RESEARCH ON MY GREAT GRANDFATHER. BUT NO ONE REMEMBERS HIM HERE.

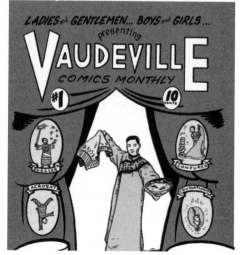

LADIES and GENTLEMEN... BOYS and GIRLS... presenting VAUDEVILLE COMICS MONTHLY #1 10 CENTS

JUGGLER   CONJURER
ACROBAT   CONTORTIONIST

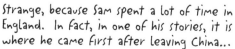

Strange, because Sam spent a lot of time in England. In fact, in one of his stories, it is where he came first after leaving China...

THE SAILORS WHO DISCOVERED LONG WANTED TO DITCH HIM IN HONG KONG--

BUT THE CAPTAIN INTERVENED--

LEAVE THE POOR CHAP ALONE! HE'S A GOOD LAD AND WANTS TO SAIL WITH US!

SO LONG REMAINED ABOARD FOR THE LENGTHY JOURNEY TO ENGLAND.

IN LONDON, HE PERFORMED HIS TRICKS ON THE DOCKS.

CROWDS OF PEOPLE WERE ENTERTAINED AND REWARDED HIM WITH SO MANY PENNIES.

THAT WAS THE FIRST TIME LONG HAD SEEN SO MUCH MONEY!

HE STAYED IN LONDON FOR A FEW YEARS MAKING AN EXCELLENT LIVING AS A YOUNG STREET PERFORMER.

THE IMMIGRATION OFFICE GRANTED APPROVAL TO LONG'S RESIDENCY APPLICATION.

OK

LADIES and GENTLEMEN, BOYS and GIRLS...

COME BACK NEXT MONTH FOR THE EXCITING CONCLUSION OF

THE LONG TACK SAM STORY!

AS FOR HIS VISA? "NO PROBLEM."

"NO PROBLEM!" WELL, I'D LIKE TO KNOW HOW HE DID IT!

WE WANT YOU!

YOU ARE MOST WELCOME.

COME ON OVER.

WE'RE WAITING FOR YOU!

FOR SAM, THE STREETS WERE PAVED WITH GOLD

He even designed a logo for himself. A long tack...

...through an "S", showing how his name alone meant money.

SUPERSAM!

"HE'S SO STRONG"

SUPER STICK GIRL

"SHE'S SO... CURIOUS"

I don't know how he did it, but while he was touring as an acrobat and magician, Sam also opened up two restaurants in London. This postcard is from Maxim's, in Soho, one of the first to serve Chinese cuisine in the city.

The second one, in Piccadilly Circus, was badly damaged in the early 1970's when the IRA (Irish Republican Army) exploded a bomb in the bank directly underneath it.

Flappers, short dresses,
the Charleston

1924

INDIA
Gandhi goes on a hunger strike to
protest Muslim-Hindu violence

POPULAR SONG:
"I'll See You In My Dreams"

FILM:
The Thief of Bagdad
with Douglas Fairbanks

The troupe goes back to
America, but things, as I
said, are changing...
Shows aren't touring the
way they used to...

MINA AND NEESA AND THE CAST OF *OUR GANG*

In America, most Vaudevillians that Sam used to share a bill with had
moved out to California to get into the movies: Cary Grant, the Marx
Brothers, Jack Benny, Charlie Chaplin, Laurel & Hardy....
Now, performers didn't have to travel all the time.

They just had to move out to California, which was very
attractive, indeed.

POLDI, CERTAINLY, IS VERY TIRED OF THE INTERNATIONAL VAUDEVILLE CIRCUIT

SHE'S LOST HER FATHER

And the road is no place for her newborn son, Frank, nicknamed "Bobbie." She wants to go home.

1924

So, in 1924, Long Tack Sam builds a second Villa Long, this time in Austria. For Poldi.

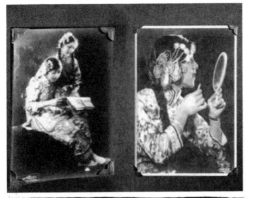

But, life costs money. The troupe has to continue to tour.
And the girls are in the show...

...and Poldi doesn't ever want to be separated from her Sam again...

Poldi leaves Bobbie with her family. He spends the first years of his life without really knowing his parents at all.

'BOBBIE' LONG
journalist, copy editor

FRANK LONG
(BOBBIE)

"They would come every few years when the show broke up for a while and buy me presents. I liked that."

I WENT TO VISIT MY UNCLE BOBBIE, IN NORTH VANCOUVER. I HAD NEVER REALLY ASKED HIM ANY QUESTIONS ABOUT HIS FAMILY, OR HAD A REAL CONVERSATION WITH HIM IN MY ADULT LIFE... TIME TO START!

I DON'T KNOW ABOUT YOU, BUT I WOULD HAVE SOME ABANDONMENT ISSUES!

BUT IN THE 16MM FILM FOOTAGE I FOUND...

...EVERYONE SEEMS TO BE HAVING A GREAT TIME—HERE'S SAM, CLOWING AROUND WITH POLDI'S RELATIVES—HER SISTER, MITZI, HER BROTHER, MAX, AND HER TINY MOTHER.

BUT IN FACT, THE FAMILY WAS RARELY HOME. IT MUST HAVE PUT A BIG STRAIN ON EVERYBODY...

I ASKED THEIR NEIGHBOR, ERNST, AGAIN, ABOUT WHAT HE REMEMBERED.

I think the marriage was good.

"I THINK THE MARRIAGE WAS GOOD. SAM LOVED HIS WIFE VERY MUCH. HE WAS A VERY DEAR MAN..."

"I don't think she was happy."

"Poldi was not happy. She was torn between Austria and America."

"Austria was too small. America was not her home."

"Austria was too small. America was not her home. She was not a happy woman."

"She was very happy to have Bobbie"

"But she was happy with her children. She was very happy to have Bobbie."

AUSTRIA, ON THE OTHER HAND, IS LIKE A VACATION FOR POLDI'S DAUGHTERS. THEY ARE FREE TO HAVE A "NORMAL" LIFE. FREE FROM THE RESTRICTIONS OF THE SHOW.

ERNST TELLS ME ALL ABOUT IT.

I was friends with Mina. Baumgertel was friends with Poldi.

"It was a wonderful time."

"They already had a car. As young people, we were going out in the evenings to coffee houses and dancing. I was friends with Mina. Baumgertel was friends with Poldi (Nee-sa). And we would all go out dancing in the evenings."

THEY MUST HAVE STILL BEEN ALL TEENAGERS THEN.

"The Vienna Woods"

THE LONG FAMILY ON THE ROAD AGAIN

WHEN BOBBIE IS FIVE, HE GETS TO GO ON THE ROAD, TOO—BUT ONLY AS AN OBSERVER!

STILL, HE'S ALWAYS GASSING IT UP, FOR HIS MOTHER. FOR THE CAMERA. TRYING TO GET SOME ATTENTION.

THESE ARE JUST A FEW HAPPY, CAREFREE MOMENTS, BUT ISN'T THAT WHAT MEMORIES ARE MADE OF? MOMENTS?

GUESS WHAT BEACH THIS IS! IT'S 1929... IT COULD BE ANYWHERE...

Waikiki!

Palm trees

RIGHT SMACK BETWEEN EAST & WEST ON THE TROUPE'S ANNUAL TRANSCONTINENTAL TOURS ARE THE ISLANDS OF HAWAII. EVERY YEAR, LONG TACK SAM PUT ON A BIG SHOW THERE.

HAWAII HAD A LARGE CHINESE COMMUNITY

MY FAMILY, WITH LONG BOARDS. (GET IT?)

I TRAVELED THERE, TOO, OF COURSE, TO MEET SOME PEOPLE WHO'D SEEN THE SHOW.

"HE WAS A MAGICIAN, AND HE WAS CHINESE. ANY CHINESE, MY AGE, WOULD REMEMBER HIM."

MARJORIE TOM & LITHEIA HALL
HONOLULU, HAWAII

"YES, THAT'S RIGHT. I REMEMBER THE BEAUTIFUL DAUGHTERS AND THE COSTUMES. EVERYBODY WENT."

MANY CHINESE IN HAWAII HAD BEEN BROUGHT OVER AS INDENTURED WORKERS. MARJORIE TOM'S FATHER WAS ONE OF THE FIRST TO PURCHASE HIS FREEDOM. LITHEIA HALL'S FATHER OWNED A STORE...

Long Tack Sam still plays in front of movies here, too, but the Chinese Association booked performances of full evening shows, to celebrate their fabulous culture.

PHONE 6055 HAWAII THEATRE BETHEL & PAUAHI Sts

COLOSSAL STAGE AND SCREEN PROGRAM!
FAREWELL TOUR!
TODAY 2:45-7:45
BY POPULAR DEMAND
EXTRA SHOWS
Tomorrow and Thursday
2:45 — 6:30 — 8:30
POSITIVELY LAST TIMES
FRIDAY

LONG TACK SAM
with his beautiful and clever daughters
MINA and NEE-SA

PRICES
MATINEES

*from the newspaper morgue of the Kameamea Library, Honolulu. Long Tack Sam had a 'farewell tour' every year!

90

I GO TO FIND **LIKO PANG**, A CHINESE HAWAIIAN MAGICIAN WHO, I WAS TOLD, HAD THE BOWL SAM USED IN HIS NOW FAMOUS <u>GOLDFISH BOWL TRICK</u>. (AND SAM'S JOCKSTRAP. WHY, I DON'T KNOW...) HE DIDN'T, BUT HE HAD STORIES.

LIKO PANG*
Describes the trick
(illustrations adapted
from a drawing by
Cyrus Leroy Baldridge in
Quicker Than the Eye by
John Mulholland)

*"Liko" means "little blossom" in the Hawaiian language

"What happened is he runs across the stage, he does a somersault, he tumbles over, and when he comes up he has a large bowl of water... with a fish. Fantastic!"

LIKO ALSO TOLD ME ABOUT HOW HARD IT WAS TO BE A CHINESE MAGICIAN IN THOSE DAYS.

HE'S AUSTRALIAN

NO, HE'S CHINESE

PART CHINESE...

ALL CHINESE...

HA! THEN HE HAD TO STRUGGLE, TOO. HE'S PPPT!!!

STRONG!

I HAVE RELATIVES IN HAWAII, TOO! (YOU KNOW I WOULD!) MY MOTHER'S SISTER, VIVIEN, AND HER HUSBAND, HANK, LIVE HERE. I HEAR VIVIEN HAS SOME THINGS THAT BELONGED TO HER GRANDFATHER.

WHEN I OPEN UP A CHEST IN HER BEDROOM, I CAN'T BELIEVE WHAT I FIND... COSTUMES FROM THE SHOW... IN BEAUTIFUL CONDITION!

A SASH

A ROBE

A GOWN

SILK THREAD

GOLD EMBROIDERY

92

NO ONE IN THE FAMILY KNEW VIVIEN HAD THESE ARTIFACTS, AND THEIR SIGNIFICANCE WAS A MYSTERY BECAUSE NO ONE HAD SEEN THE SHOW. SHE JUST THOUGHT THEY WERE SOME COSTUMES OF HER MOTHER'S, WITH SENTIMENTAL VALUE (GRANNY LOVED COSTUME PARTIES!)

THE CHINESE OPERA, *PEONY PRINCESS*, HAD RECENTLY PLAYED IN NYC, AND THERE WAS A LOT OF INFORMATION FLOATING AROUND ABOUT THE COSTUMES OF THIS ERA, MADE BY THE MASTER WEAVERS OF SUCHOW. LONG TACK SAM HAD HIS COSTUMES AND BACKDROPS MADE FROM THERE, TOO. IT TOOK <u>TWO</u> <u>YEARS</u> FOR THEM TO GET AN ORDER READY. ACROBATS WERE VERY HARD ON THEIR CLOTHING! LOTS OF WEAR AND TEAR!

Silkworms

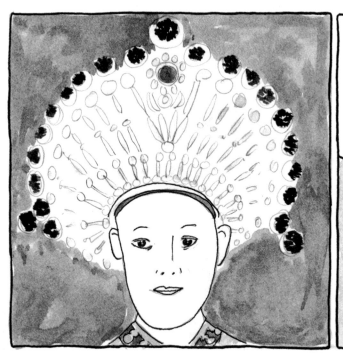

THE BALLS ON THE HEADRESSES REPRESENTED THAT PERSON'S POSITION IN HEAVEN, BY THEIR COLOR AND PLACEMENT.

I FIND OTHER ARTIFACTS FROM THE SHOW AT MY AUNT'S. PARTS FROM A BOW AND ARROW ROUTINE...

...HIS MAGIC FEATHER

...AND, MY FAVORITE...MORE STORIES!

MY UNCLE USED TO BE A GENERAL IN THE USMC, AND WAS REPRESENTING THEM AT AN ADVERTISING FUNCTION WHERE GEORGE BURNS WAS ACCEPTING AN AWARD FOR A SPOT HE DID FOR THE GLENDALE BANK...

"HE WAS VERY POPULAR AT THAT TIME...
I SAT ON THE DAIS WITH HIM AND ASKED IF HE RECALLED LONG TACK SAM, THE FATHER OF MY MOTHER-IN-LAW. WITH THAT, HE VIRTUALLY

GENERAL HENRY STACKPOLE
COCO HEAD, HAWAII

ROSE OUT OF HIS CHAIR, GRABBED MY ARM AND SAID:

THE GREATEST VAUDEVILLE ACT I'VE EVER SEEN! HIS ACROBATICS WERE THE PIECE DE RESISTANCE! HE WAS A GREAT MAGICIAN! HE HAD TWO BEAUTIFUL DAUGHTERS! THEY WERE SMASHING!"

HE WAS TALKING ABOUT MINA AND NEESA, WHO HAD BECOME THE MAINSTAY OF THE ACT...

"LIKE MOTHER, LIKE DAUGHTERS"

MINA PLAYING THE UKULELE

MINA AND NEESA, PLAYING MINI-GOLF WITH THEIR DAD

AS THEIR FATHER SAID:
"THEY DO THE WORK AND I GET THE MONEY!"

Sam, because he traveled so fluidly, back and forth, between Europe, the Americas and Asia, was one of the first conduits of Western magic to the East. For instance, in 1930, the tune "The Doll Dance", came out in the U.S. and was immediately incorporated into a magic act, where a woman appears from a little dollhouse. Everyone was doing this act! Sam was performing it in China that very same year!

*Thanks to Gordon Bean, librarian at the Magic Castle in Los Angeles, for sleuthing this out for me!

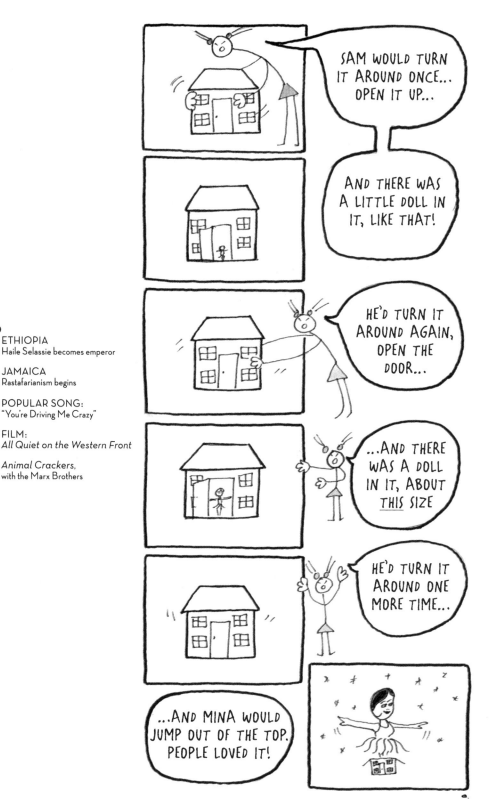

ETHIOPIA
Haile Selassie becomes emperor

JAMAICA
Rastafarianism begins

POPULAR SONG:
"You're Driving Me Crazy"

FILM:
All Quiet on the Western Front

Animal Crackers,
with the Marx Brothers

GRANNY TOLD ME HOW SHE'D TRAINED AS A BALLERINA

SHE ALSO PLAYED THE SAXOPHONE

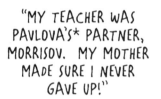

"MY TEACHER WAS PAVLOVA'S* PARTNER, MORRISOV. MY MOTHER MADE SURE I NEVER GAVE UP!"

*PAVLOVA WAS A RUSSIAN BALLERINA. "DAINTINESS & FRAGILITY WERE HER GREATEST ASSETS." SHE WAS SO POPULAR IN AUSTRALIA THAT THEY CREATED A DESSERT AFTER HER. HERE'S HOW YOU MAKE IT.

PAVLOVA

- MAKE A MERINGUE (8 EGG WHITES, SOME SUGAR, BEAT UNTIL STIFF PEAKS FORM)
- BAKE IN 400F OVEN UNTIL LIGHT BROWN (APPROX. 20 MINUTES)
- WHIP CREAM, WITH SUGAR/LIQUEUR TO TASTE
- CUT UP FRUIT OF YOUR CHOICE
- TAKE MERINGUE OUT OF OVEN AND COOL
- FILL WITH WHIP CREAM AND TOP WITH FRUIT! IT'S DELICIOUS!

POLDI PLAYED THE VIOLIN, SANG AND DID CONTORTIONS

"NEESA WAS VERY GOOD"

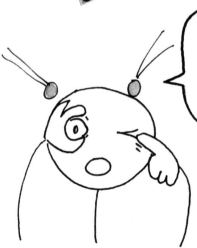

SINGING?

YES

ENGLISH SONGS

WESTERN SONGS?

LIKE JOHANN STRAUSS

STRAUSS?

YES, WE LIKE THAT
-N. W.YAO

PEOPLE LIKED THEIR MIX OF EASTERN AND WESTERN CULTURES

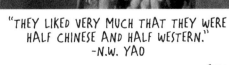

"THEY LIKED VERY MUCH THAT THEY WERE HALF CHINESE AND HALF WESTERN."
-N.W. YAO

*LONG TACK SAM IS STANDING TWO STAIRS HIGHER THAN HIS DAUGHTERS... WHO ARE ONLY 5'2"

FROM PARISIAN TOE-DANCE TO APACHE WAR DANCE, IF IT WAS ENTERTAINING, IT WAS IN THE SHOW...

I FOUND SOME LETTERS SAM WROTE WHILE HE WAS TRAVELING AROUND THE WORLD, IN THE DYING DAYS OF VAUDEVILLE

SAM IN CHINA

Dear Willie,
Your letter from March 21 received and I sure was glad to hear from you.
It sure must be bad in the States now for vaudeville, as your letter states.
How is everything going with you? We all hope you are enjoying the best of health and are enjoying a good season...

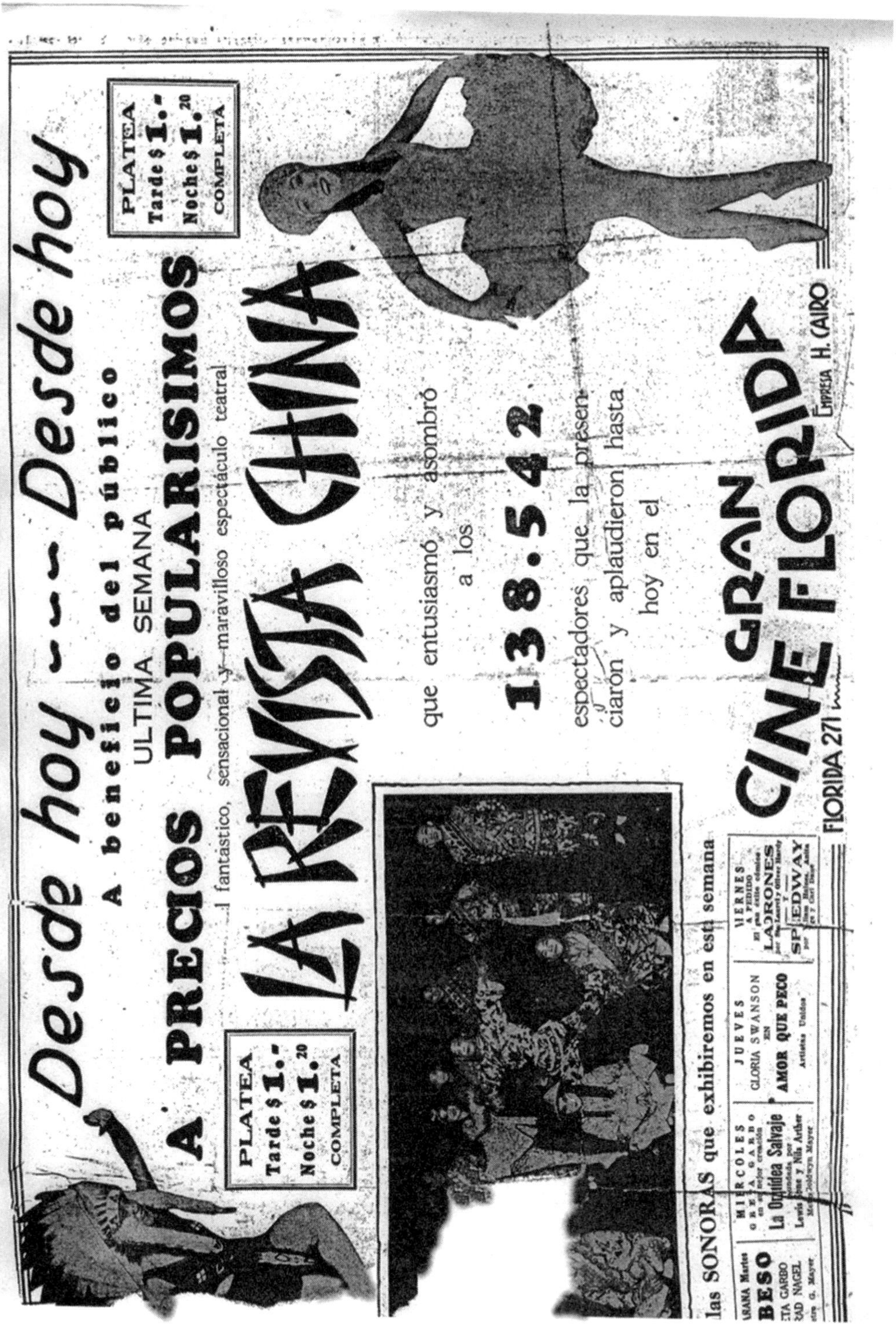

Desde hoy ~~~ Desde hoy ~~~ Desde hoy
A beneficio del público
ULTIMA SEMANA
A PRECIOS POPULARISIMOS
PLATEA
Tarde $ 1.-
Noche $ 1.20
COMPLETA
PLATEA
Tarde $ 1.-
Noche $ 1.20
COMPLETA
l fantástico, sensacional y maravilloso espectáculo teatral
LA REVISTA CHINA
que entusiasmó y asombró
a los
138.542
espectadores que la presenciaron y aplaudieron hasta
hoy en el
GRAN
CINE FLORIDA
FLORIDA 271
EMPRESA H. CAIRO
las SONORAS que exhibiremos en esta semana
BESO
MIERCOLES
GRETA GARBO
La Orquídea Salvaje
JUEVES
GLORIA SWANSON
EN
AMOR QUE PECO
Artistas Unidos
VIERNES
A PEDIDO
LADRONES
SPEEDWAY

Longs in Rio

Dear Willie,*

Leaving tomorrow for Rio—
Teatro Odeon then Sao Paolo.
We sail June 17th on the S.S.
American Legion. We played
7 weeks at the Cine Florida,
breaking house records.

(*"Willie" was William Goldston, English
magician and trick builder)

Longs in New Zealand

Dear Willie,

Just a few lines to let you know
at present we are touring Java.
After a successful engagement
in Manila. Haven't forgotten
about the shadow thing you
asked me to get for you...
Will head to Singapore from
Batavia, so, if you have time,
drop me a line at the Capitol
Theatre.

Show promo

Gran Cine Florida

LOTS OF TRAVELING! IT'S TIME TO GO BACK TO AUSTRIA FOR A LITTLE VACATION EACH SUMMER!*

*before air-conditioning, Vaudeville houses closed down in the heat

VILLA LONG
LINZ, AUSTRIA

IT'S A VERY DIFFERENT HOLIDAY AT HOME IN AUSTRIA AT THE END OF THE 1920'S. HITLER IS NOT GOING TO BE ELECTED CHANCELLOR OF GERMANY UNTIL 1933, BUT HE IS ON THE POLITICAL LANDSCAPE BEFORE THAT. ABOVE, YOU CAN SEE MY GRANDMOTHER MAKING FUN OF THE GOOSESTEPPING STYLE OF THE NATIONAL SOCIALISTS—NAZIS—BUT HITLER IS ABOUT TO BECOME A VERY DANGEROUS FORCE.

FELIX THE CAT

CHARLIE CHAPLIN

CHARLIE RIVAL

ADOLPH HITLER

BOBBIE LONG

MY THEORY IS, WHILE MINA WAS MIMICKING HITLER, HITLER WAS MIMICKING THE MOST POPULAR ENTERTAINER OF THE TIME—CHARLIE CHAPLIN, BY GROWING A LITTLE MOUSTACHE TO TRY AND MAKE HIMSELF MORE LIKEABLE. EVERYBODY WAS MIMICKING CHAPLIN: LONG TACK SAM TOURED WITH A CHAPLIN IMPERSONATOR—CHARLIE RIVAL. LITTLE BOBBIE LONG DRESSED UP LIKE CHAPLIN. EVEN FELIX THE CAT DID CHAPLIN.

HERE IS HITLER, THE CHAPLIN IMPERSONATOR, VISITING A BOYS' SCHOOL IN LINZ. BEHIND HIM, IN THE SHADOWS, STANDS THE EURASIAN BOBBIE LONG, NOT A WELCOME PART OF HITLER'S LONG TERM PLANS. IF EVERYTHING WORKED OUT, LINZ WAS GOING TO BE THE CAPITOL OF THE THIRD REICH.

BERLIN

AGAIN, THERE IS GREAT DEPRESSION AND POVERTY IN GERMANY, AND THESE ELEMENTS OFTEN BREED INTOLERANCE.

AT THE SAME TIME, VAUDEVILLE, BURLESQUE, NIGHTCLUBS WERE AT THEIR HEIGHT IN CITIES LIKE BERLIN.

FASCISM IS ON THE RISE

Above, Poldi fits right in, playing tourist in Berlin....

...but her two daughters are under a different kind of scrutiny...

SCALA

· DIE ·
VARIETÉ·
BÜHNE

* 22
...ERSTR...N

Leineweber
DAS HAUS DAS JEDEN ANZIEHT

The Long Tack Sam Troupe plays the Scala Theatre. The reviews are mixed, because the girls are. Now, they are not <u>Chinese</u> enough. What used to work in their favor—their cross-cultural heritage and hybrid act—now works against them. The new Germany demands purity of race and of form.

Sam worries about his girls.

He keeps them under his watchful eye.

"We were brought up very strict. My father was VERY VERY strict. Because, he said, "First of all, you're in showbusiness. Second, you're Eurasian," which at the time, was not so hot. "And that's why I'm bringing you up double strict.""

MINA 1987

1934

"We weren't allowed to mix up with too many people. I wasn't allowed to go out by myself. I was 25 years old."

AS LONG AS I CAN REMEMBER, GROWING UP, MY GRANDMOTHER ALWAYS MADE A FUSS ABOUT ME BEING EURASIAN AND HOW SPECIAL AND WONDERFUL THAT WAS—TO BE PART OF MANY CULTURES. MAYBE THAT HELPED ME WHEN PEOPLE—KIDS MAINLY—WOULD ASK ME WHERE I WAS FROM. WHAT WAS I? I WANTED TO TELL THEM. I THOUGHT IT WAS INTERESTING. I DIDN'T KNOW GRANNY DIDN'T WANT ME TO HAVE THE COMPLEX SHE HAD FROM GROWING UP IN A WORLD WHERE, SOMETIMES, IT WAS SEEN AS WRONG.

15

5

The troupe goes to America to escape the European blues.
Don't they call the U.S. the melting pot of culture?

But after the Stock Market Crash of 1929

...and the Dust Bowl years of the Dirty '30's...

the U.S. is reeling from its own Depression.

More than ever, America needs its escapist entertainment.

LONG TACK SAM PUTS ON HIS BIG SHOW IN HARD TIMES AND PLIES HIS TRADE IN FRONT OF THE MOVIES.

GETTING A GIG IN A VAUDEVILLE SHOW WAS STILL ONE OF THE BEST JOBS IN TOWN! HERE ARE SOME SNAPSHOTS I RECEIVED FROM BADONNA KAHN*, WHO WAS A 16-YEAR-OLD CHORUS GIRL WHEN SHE PERFORMED WITH MY FAMILY IN 1932. MY GRANDMOTHER WROTE TO HER FOR YEARS.

*Her daughter, Karen, somehow found me on the internet and got us in touch. Amazing!

GOD BLESS THE INTERNET

SMALL WORLD

BADONNA (RIGHT)
MINA (MIDDLE)
I DON'T KNOW YET (LEFT)

AL CAPONE

IT WAS PROHIBITION. NEESA WAS DATING AL CAPONE, THE NOTORIOUS GANGSTER. OR, MAYBE, THAT'S JUST ANOTHER STORY.

NOT EVERYONE WAS SUFFERING DURING THE DEPRESSION. THE POOR GOT POORER, MAINLY, BUT A LOT OF INDUSTRIALISTS PROFITED FROM THE WAR IN EUROPE THAT WAS GEARING UP.

1932 is the year that Sam created a dance for Syd Graumann, starring his daughter, Mina, to be performed in front of the new Joan Crawford vehicle, *Rain*, which opened at his Chinese Theatre in Hollywood. Graumann is another entrepeneur who understood the allure of the Middle Kingdom.

GRAUMANN'S THEATRE

Loretta Young and Long Tack Sam

The White Parade and Long Tack Sam

Jean Harlow and Long Tack Sam

The Girl from Missouri and Long Tack Sam ad

MOVIES ARE THE PREDOMINANT FORM OF ENTERTAINMENT IN AMERICA NOW AND HOLLYWOOD IS RAPIDLY FILLING UP WITH NEW IMMIGRANTS FROM AN INCREASINGLY HOSTILE EUROPE.

October, 1930

THE·SPHINX

AN INDEPENDENT MAGAZINE FOR MAGICIANS
VOLUME XXIX, NUMBER EIGHT

October, 1930

303

Freezing Ice In The Hand

By LONG TACK SAM

A Favorite Feat with the Magicians of China

This is a favorite trick of Chinese magicians and is very old though, I believe, entirely unknown to the performers of other countries. The effect depends upon the trick being worked neatly and also it depends upon the assurance of the magician but this is very largely true, of course, of every bit of magic either Occidental or Oriental. The Chinese magician is taught while an apprentice to learn the routine and patter of a trick thoroughly and not to vary its performance. Unless every move is the result of studied effort the trick cannot have its full effect.

With a bow to Lu Tsu Bing, the patron saint of the Chinese magician, I begin. The effect is good not only because it is mystifying but because it is surprising. From a bowl filled with water the magician dips out a handful and changes the water to a small block of ice. The hottest weather and the most iceless small town are no hinderance.

The ice is made from a heavy colorless piece of plate glass chipped to look like an ice block. The ice should be about an inch and one-quarter thick. It will be found that it can be palmed like a billiard ball and must therefore have no sharp edges.

In performing the trick the magician has the bowl of water on a small table behind which he stands. Any small opaque bowl will do. In his right hand he palms the ice. He shows the left hand empty and pulls up the right sleeve. Chinese sleeves have tight cuffs. The

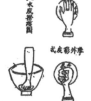

From an Old Chinese Book

sleeves are pulled up, in effect, to keep them out of the water but, in reality, as a means of showing the hands empty. The left hand is again shown empty after the sleeve is pulled up and the ice by a change over palm is then palmed in the left hand. The right hand is shown empty and the left sleeve pulled up the arm. All this is done without apparently doing anything except protect the sleeves from getting wet and yet is done with slow enough motions so that the audience will not suspect that either hand holds anything.

The left hand is now palming the ice. The right hand is cupped and dipped into the water and a handful is brought out and, with a flourish, poured back into the bowl. This should be done so as to make as big a show as possible of the quantity of the water you dip up. This is done several times. Finally the motion of dipping is gone through again

but no water is taken up and this time water apparently is poured into the other hand. The left hand is closed around the ice and held thumb up so that the water seemingly goes into the hole made by the curved thumb and first finger. Again apparently water is poured into the hand. There will be enough water on the right hand from its previous wettings to shake off a few drops after giving the effect of filling the left hand.

The left hand now seemingly squeezes the water so that it forms the ice block and slowly opens it revealing the ice. The ice naturally is thought to be cold and you must remember to give the effeect of its freezing your hand. To do that you put it first on one hand and then on the other each time rubbing the fingers of the free hand over the palm of that hand. This should not be over done. It is well to try with a piece of real ice to see what you would naturally do. The ice is finally dropped into the bowl of water. The Chinese magician then walks amongst his audience with the bowl so that the ice may be seen. A piece of chipped glass looks like ice at any time but in the water it may be shown with safty right among the audience.

As I said before this is an old effect in China but it is very effective and the audiences like it. It is pretty safe to say a trick found to be effective in one part of the world can be used to advantage in any other part.

SAM IS NOT JUST AN ENTERTAINER, MAKING A BUCK. HE IS ALSO A LOVER OF MAGIC. HERE HE SHARES A TRICK WITH OTHER CONJURERS—BOTH AMATEUR AND PROFESSIONAL—IN THE MAGICIAN'S JOURNAL, *THE SPHINX*.

The girls get screen-tested for parts in movies like *The Good Earth*...

...but they are rejected, told they are "too pretty" to play Chinese girls.

For the most part, Chinese were portrayed in movies as bandits, opium smokers...

...asexual murderers and all-round bad guys. Talk about bad press!

Long Tack Sam had built a career on presenting a beautiful show with beautiful performers, but that's not how people wanted to see Chinese.

Sam spent his whole life adjusting to his audience, but now he puts his foot down. He is <u>NOT</u> going Hollywood, and neither are his daughters. He was kissing their careers good-bye.

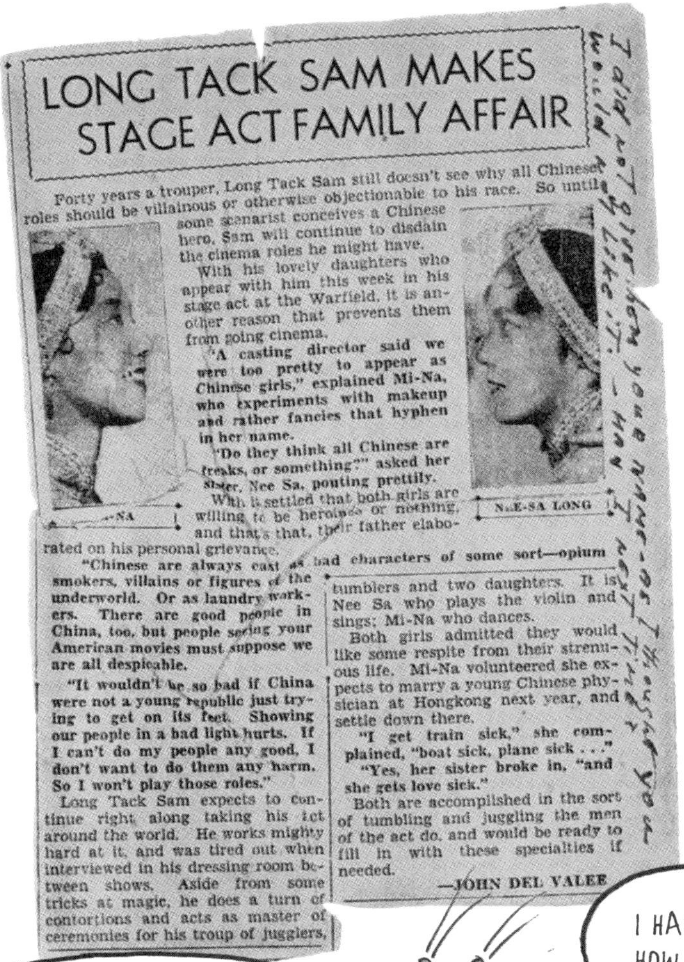

LONG TACK SAM MAKES STAGE ACT FAMILY AFFAIR

Forty years a trouper, Long Tack Sam still doesn't see why all Chinese roles should be villainous or otherwise objectionable to his race. So until some scenarist conceives a Chinese hero, Sam will continue to disdain the cinema roles he might have.

With his lovely daughters who appear with him this week in his stage act at the Warfield, it is another reason that prevents them from going cinema.

"A casting director said we were too pretty to appear as Chinese girls," explained Mi-Na, who experiments with makeup and rather fancies that hyphen in her name.

"Do they think all Chinese are freaks, or something?" asked her sister, Nee Sa, pouting prettily.

...-NA

NEE-SA LONG

With it settled that both girls are willing to be heroines or nothing, and that's that, their father elaborated on his personal grievance.

"Chinese are always cast as bad characters of some sort—opium smokers, villains or figures of the underworld. Or as laundry workers. There are good people in China, too, but people seeing your American movies must suppose we are all despicable.

"It wouldn't be so bad if China were not a young republic just trying to get on its feet. Showing our people in a bad light hurts. If I can't do my people any good, I don't want to do them any harm. So I won't play those roles."

Long Tack Sam expects to continue right along taking his act around the world. He works mighty hard at it, and was tired out when interviewed in his dressing room between shows. Aside from some tricks at magic, he does a turn of contortions and acts as master of ceremonies for his troup of jugglers, tumblers and two daughters. It is Nee Sa who plays the violin and sings; Mi-Na who dances.

Both girls admitted they would like some respite from their strenuous life. Mi-Na volunteered she expects to marry a young Chinese physician at Hongkong next year, and settle down there.

"I get train sick," she complained, "boat sick, plane sick . . ."

"Yes, her sister broke in, "and she gets love sick."

Both are accomplished in the sort of tumbling and juggling the men of the act do, and would be ready to fill in with these specialties if needed.

—JOHN DEL VALEE

I did not give them your name—as I thought you
would like it.

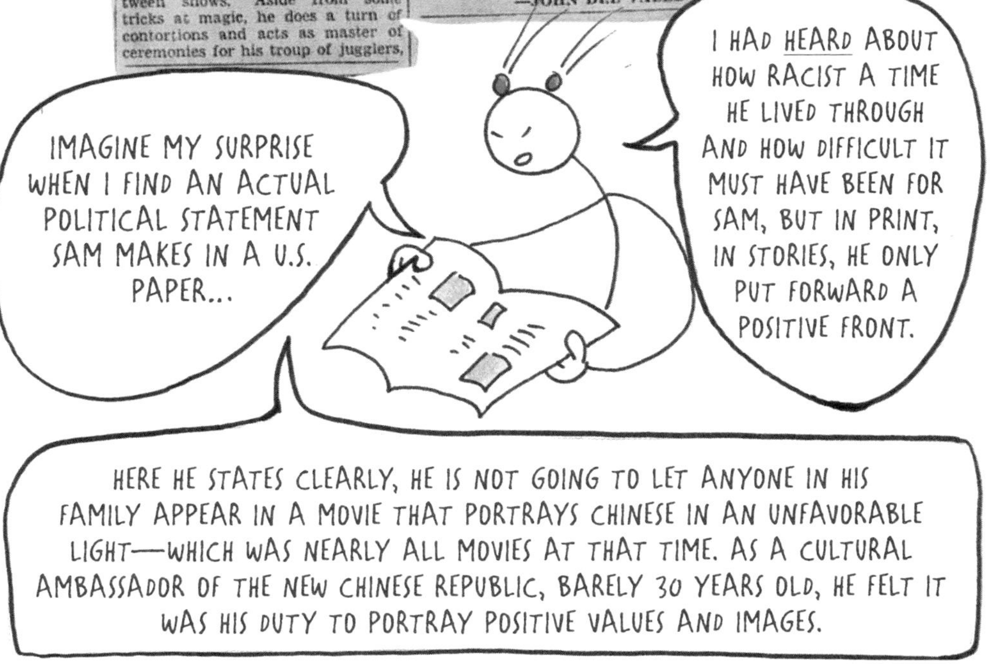
IMAGINE MY SURPRISE WHEN I FIND AN ACTUAL POLITICAL STATEMENT SAM MAKES IN A U.S. PAPER...
I HAD HEARD ABOUT HOW RACIST A TIME HE LIVED THROUGH AND HOW DIFFICULT IT MUST HAVE BEEN FOR SAM, BUT IN PRINT, IN STORIES, HE ONLY PUT FORWARD A POSITIVE FRONT.
HERE HE STATES CLEARLY, HE IS NOT GOING TO LET ANYONE IN HIS FAMILY APPEAR IN A MOVIE THAT PORTRAYS CHINESE IN AN UNFAVORABLE LIGHT—WHICH WAS NEARLY ALL MOVIES AT THAT TIME. AS A CULTURAL AMBASSADOR OF THE NEW CHINESE REPUBLIC, BARELY 30 YEARS OLD, HE FELT IT WAS HIS DUTY TO PORTRAY POSITIVE VALUES AND IMAGES.

MORE TROUBLE ON THE HORIZON

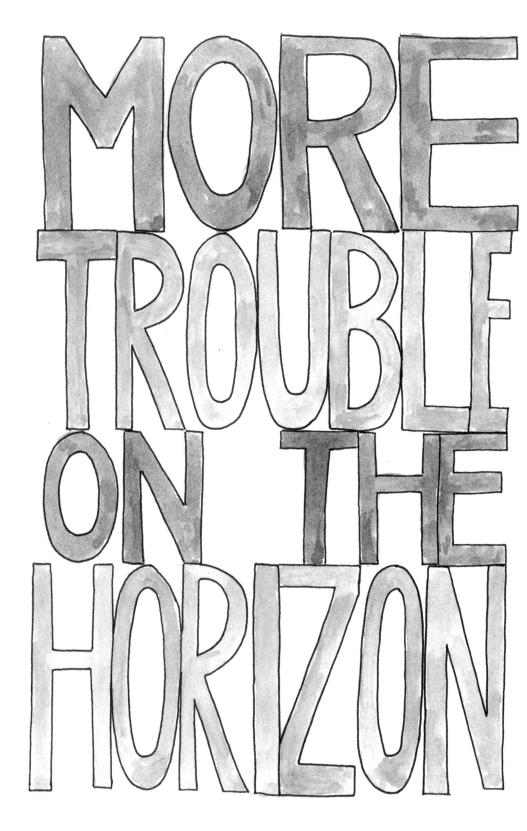

THE TROUPE WOULD NORMALLY DO THE ORPHEUM CIRCUIT THAT CROSSED THE BORDER INTO CANADA, BUT IN 1932, CANADA'S CHINESE IMMIGRATION ACT AND THE U.S.'S CHINESE EXCLUSION ACT MADE TRAVELING FAR MORE DIFFICULT EVEN THOUGH THERE WAS SPECIAL DISPENSATION FOR ENTERTAINERS.

LOOK HOW CLOSE YOU USED TO BE ABLE TO GET TO NIAGARA FALLS!

BUT POLDI WASN'T UP TO MANAGING THE TROUPE ANYMORE...

PEOPLE WHO KNEW HER SAID "SOMETHING WAS NOT RIGHT."

SO, LONG TACK SAM AGREES TO CREATE A REVIEW FOR THE IMPRESARIOS, FANCHON AND MARCO, WHO BRING THEM UP THE WEST COAST. THE SHOW IS CALLED "SHANGHAI."

THEY PERFORMED "SHANGHAI" IN FRONT OF THE OMINOUSLY-NAMED WILLIAM POWELL VEHICLE, *ONE WAY PASSAGE*, AT THE ORPHEUM THEATER IN VANCOUVER.

INTERESTINGLY, BACK IN 1912, SAM HELD RETURN TIX FOR ANOTHER ILL-FATED OCEAN LINER—THE *TITANIC*. NEEDLESS TO SAY, HE DIDN'T GET TO USE THEM!

SAM, NEE-SA AND MI-NA HANGING OUT BEHIND THEATRE

VAUDEVILLE IS LIKE A SAUSAGE FACTORY AT THIS POINT. ACTS BEFORE MOVIES, 5 TIMES A DAY, AND LONG TACK SAM'S ACT WAS EXTREMELY TAXING. THE GIRLS ARE STILL YOUNG ENOUGH TO KEEP UP THE PACE... BUT SAM IS REALLY FEELING HIS YEARS. HE'S 57 NOW. HIS GIRLS ARE IN THEIR EARLY 20'S. APPARENTLY, HE HAD SPURS ON HIS SPINE AND WAS IN CONSTANT PAIN!

LIFE IS STRANGE. HAD THEY WANTED TO, SAM AND POLDI WOULDN'T HAVE BEEN ALLOWED TO STAY IN CANADA IN 1932, BUT MINA MOVED HERE, MANY YEARS LATER. (SHE HAD MENTIONED SHE PLAYED THE ORPHEUM—BUT NOT WHAT SHE WAS DOING!!) AND HER BROTHER, BOBBBIE, LIVED HERE... IN 1999...

"SAM HAD A HUGE LUMP ON HIS BACK. HIS VERTEBRAE WAS SORT OF MALFORMED HERE, FROM ALL THE ACROBATICS HE DID..."

BOBBIE, AS I SAID, WAS NEVER PART OF THE ACT. BUT HE COULD GIVE ME A PRETTY GOOD TIMELINE OF WHAT HAPPENED AS THE TOUR STARTED WINDING DOWN...

MINA, "CLOWNING AROUND"

MINA OPENS A DANCE STUDIO IN SHANGHAI... AND STARTS WRITING A COLUMN FOR THE CHINA NEWS ESPOUSING FEMALE EMANCIPATION THROUGH PHYSICAL FITNESS! EXERCISE FOR CHINA'S THEN 200 MILLION WOMEN! SHE GIVES UP HER JOB TO JOIN THE RED CROSS WHEN THE JAPANESE INVADE.

I'M VERY PROUD OF MY GRANDMOTHER!!

For Strong Physique ... ong Women Is Described

TALENTED

Eventually, Mina abandons show business and marries my grandfather, Ernest To, who belongs to three generations of doctors (you should hear HIS side's story).

GRANDPA'S FAMILY DID NOT APPROVE OF THE UNION, FOR ALL THE REASONS—GRANNY WAS A SHOWGIRL... AND EURASIAN.

LONG TACK SAM JUST WANTED HER TO MARRY SOMEONE CHINESE, OR SO SHE THOUGHT...

BUT GRANDPA WAS SMITTEN! (THOUGH HE TOLD ME HE USED TO GO ON DATES WITH BOTH SISTERS, BEFORE HE MADE UP HIS MIND...)

Supported by his entire company of Oriental Mystery Makers & China's most beautiful girl...

Miss NEE SA LONG

NEESA TRIES HER HAND AT MANAGING THE SHOW FOR A WHILE...

...BUT ALSO JUMPS SHIP TO MARRY THE WEALTHY SHANGHAI INDUSTRIALIST, N. C. YAO

1936

ENGLAND
King Edward VIII abdicates to marry twice divorced American Wallis Simpson

BBC makes first television broadcast

GERMANY
Berlin Olympics

Jesse Owens shatters long jump record

Germany occupies Rhineland

SPAIN
Civil War begins

U.S.A.
LIFE Magazine launched

Pan Am offers first transpacific service

FILM:
Modern Times by Charlie Chaplin

1937

CHINA
Japan attacks

FILM:
Snow White and the Seven Dwarfs, first animated feature

ART:
Picasso paints *Guernica*

1937
POPULAR SONG:
"Our Love Is Here to Stay,"
by George Gershwin

U.S.A.
George Gershwin dies
of a brain tumor

Sam wants something better for his daughters than a life on the road. He wants them to marry into respectable, CHINESE families...

BUT NEITHER HE NOR POLDI GO TO EITHER OF HIS DAUGHTER'S WEDDINGS!

THE SHOW IS OVER. THE FAMILY SPLITS UP.

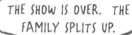

BOBBIE'S FIFTEEN. SCHOOL'S OVER. SAM AND POLDI BRING HIM FROM ENGLAND BACK TO AUSTRIA—TO LINZ AND VILLA LONG. THEY COULD NOT HAVE PICKED A WORSE TIME!

Sam and Poldi return to England to get Bobbie...

WAR BREAKS OUT

Germany invades Poland. Austria is automatically drawn in.

YOU'D THINK THE LONGS WOULD JUST HIGH-TAIL IT OUT OF THERE, WOULDN'T YOU?

1938

MIDDLE EAST
Oil found in Saudi Arabia

GERMANY
Kristallnacht

U.S.A.
Superman character premieres in *Action Comics*

1939

EUROPE
SEPT 1:
Hitler invades Poland

SEPT 3:
Britain declares war on Germany

POPULAR SONG:
"Heaven Can Wait"

FILM:
Gone With the Wind
The Wizard of Oz
both nominated for an Academy Award, *GWTW* wins

THE LONGS CAN'T GO BACK TO ENGLAND BECAUSE OF POLDI'S NATIONALITY. AUSTRIA WAS NOW PART OF GERMANY. POLDI WAS CONSIDERED AN ENEMY ALIEN, EVEN THOUGH SHE HAD A CHINESE PASSPORT. THE NAZIS WENT THROUGH OVER 400 YEARS OF CHURCH RECORDS TO TRY AND FIND JEWISH ANCESTRY. HOW LONG BEFORE THEY STARTED TO ASK OTHER QUESTIONS ABOUT RACE AND CULTURE?! SAM AND POLDI GRAB BOBBIE AND HEAD DOWN TO ITALY....

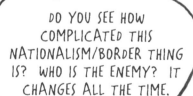

DO YOU SEE HOW COMPLICATED THIS NATIONALISM/BORDER THING IS? WHO IS THE ENEMY? IT CHANGES ALL THE TIME.

SAM WITH POLDI'S COUSIN, AN AUSTRIAN ARMY OFFICER

THESE PICTURES SHOW THE WELL-HEELED LONGS ENJOYING THEMSELVES IN ITALY (MILAN, TO BE PRECISE)—SEEING THE SIGHTS, OUT IN CAFES...

BUT THEY ARE EXILES ON THE RUN...

WAR

MUSSOLINI, THE POPULIST ITALIAN LEADER, HAS THROWN HIS FASCIST SUPPORT BEHIND HITLER. ITALY IS DRAWN INTO THE WAR.

Fascism: [Italian] fascismo, from fascio, ital. *group*, from Late Latin fascium, from Latin, *bundle*.

LUCKILY, THE LONGS HAVE THE FUNDS AND THE FRIENDS TO HELP GET THEM OUT OF EUROPE. THEY TAKE A BOAT TO AMERICA, WHICH IS NOT YET IN THE WAR.

ANOTHER SNAPSHOT OF SAM'S TROUBLED TIMES...

IN JACKIE FLOSSO'S MAGIC SHOP, IN NYC, MAGICIAN STANLEY PALM PULLS OUT AN ARTICLE THAT APPEARED IN THE 1940 *WORLD NEWS*. SAM HAD JUST LANDED IN AMERICA FROM FLEEING EUROPE. HE READS IT...

STANLEY PALM'S HANDS IN FLOSSO & HORNMANN'S MAGIC SHOP

"He says he is on his way to China, stopping off to buy soap for relatives, in Austria, who are without any amenities. All he wants is a normal life for his son... a life without show business."

RIGHT. WELL, THAT KIND OF LIFE IS UNTHINKABLE FOR LONG TACK SAM.

THE AMERICAN MUSEUM OF MAGIC IN MARSHALL, MICHIGAN, IS WHERE I FIND OUT HOW SAM AND POLDI SPENT THAT AUGUST IN NEW YORK CITY.

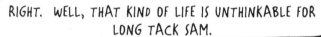

AMERICAN MUSEUM OF MAGIC MARSHALL, MICHIGAN

*Remember Elaine Lund? In her basement, filed year by year, is every event tht took place in magic, in America, in the 20th century!

The Society of American Magicians (S.A.M.) puts on a benefit dinner and show for Long Tack Sam and Poldi. (I wonder what they are watching?)

YOU CAN SEE FROM THESE PICTURES HOW POLDI'S NERVES ARE BEGINNING TO FRAY! WELL, WHOSE WOULDN'T?

Shanghai

THEY CAN'T STAY IN AMERICA (VISA ISSUES AGAIN). THE ONLY PLACE LEFT TO GO IS BACK TO CHINA, SAM'S HOMELAND, AND TO SHANGHAI, ONE OF THE FEW OPEN CITIES LEFT IN THE WORLD.

MANCHURIAN BORDER

SAM BACK IN SHANGHAI

THINGS AREN'T COMPLETELY NORMAL IN SHANGHAI, EITHER. THERE HAVE BEEN SKIRMISHES WITH THE JAPANESE AROUND THE MANCHURIAN BORDER, BUT THE JAPANESE HAVE BEEN INSINUATING THEIR WAY INTO CHINA FOR SUCH A LONG TIME, PEOPLE ARE ALMOST USED TO IT.

IT STILL FEELS SAFER THAN THE WAR IN EUROPE

MAX AND SAM

EDWIN AND MAX

Many magicians and friends pass through—most notably Max Malini. Perhaps the only person in magic shorter than Sam (he's on a step, here)

Here is Max with Sam's dear friend, Edwin Dearn, an amateur magician and historian.

Edwin Dearn and Sam in the 'library'

I GOT THESE PICTURES FROM EDWIN'S SON, ARTHUR, WHO LIVES IN AUSTRALIA. I DROPPED IN ON HIM WHEN I WAS VISITING RELATIVES. I HAD BEEN TRYING FOR YEARS TO GET IN TOUCH WITH HIM. HE HAD SOME DIFFICULT MEMORIES OF CHINA. HIS WIFE, MARILYN, RESCUES POSSUMS FROM BUSHFIRES.

The Dearns become the Longs closest companions.

BUT ONCE AGAIN, SAM'S TIMING IS TERRIBLY WRONG. LESS THAN A MONTH AFTER THESE PHOTOS ARE TAKEN...

September, 1940: the Japanese invade Shanghai. The Dearns—being British and since Britain is at war with Germany and Japan has joined sides with the Axis powers in Europe—are put in camps for 3 years. Sam looks after the Dearns' possessions. (After the war, the Dearns move to Australia. Arthur will never set foot in China again.)

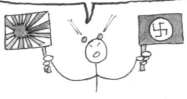

WHEN JAPAN JOINS SIDES WITH GERMANY, THEY FORMALLY DECLARE WAR ON CHINA

* Ironic that the Nazis chose the Swastika, a Buddhist symbol, as their main icon. In Sanskrit it means "conducive to well-being." In China and Japan it denotes "plurality and abundance."

THE SAME THING THAT KEPT THE LONGS OUT OF ENGLAND AND AMERICA SAVES THEM IN THIS PARTICULAR INSTANCE—POLDI'S AUSTRIAN NATIONALITY AND GERMAN LANGUAGE.

SAM MAGICALLY ESCAPES PERSECUTION ONCE AGAIN.

POLDI, WRITING A LETTER HOME

A WAR STORY

Sam was standing outside one of his theaters when the Japanese military came to arrest him.

He told them that he had just seen Long Tack Sam go inside.

The soldiers went looking for him and Long Tack Sam escaped.

John Nicholls Booth is a reverend, magician, writer, historian and raconteur who met Long Tack Sam just after the war, in Shanghai, at the Press Club in the 'Shanghai Mansions.' He tells this story of what Sam told him.

John Booth, Long Beach, CA, 1999

"There was this British chief of police—a big, tall man—who was being tortured* by the Japanese Army. Everyone in the Quarter** could hear the screams of this man as he was being tortured to death. Finally, the screaming stopped, and everyone breathed a sigh of relief. There was only silence in the air."

HE SAID HE'D NEVER BE ABLE TO FORGET THE EXPRESSION ON MY GREAT-GRANDFATHER'S FACE AS HE TOLD THIS STORY. BUT HE COULDN'T DESCRIBE IT TO ME.

* The Japanese army had a reputation during WWII not only for their ruthless treatment of enemy soldiers and civilians but also their harsh treatment of their own troops.

** There were 3 "quarters" in pre war Shanghai. The International Settlement (British, American, Russian), the French Concession, and the Chinese Section.

1945 Shanghai, alive and well in 1999

130

U.S.S. *ARIZONA* Dec. 7, 1941

WITH THE BOMBING OF THE U.S. MILITARY BASE ON HAWAII'S PEARL HARBOR, THE AMERICANS ARE DRAWN INTO THE WAR. WWII IS OFFICIALLY ALL OVER THE GLOBE NOW AND THE WAR IN THE PACIFIC WAS TO LAST LONG AFTER THE EUROPEAN PEACE IS MADE...

1941

EUROPE
Germany invades Russia,
20 million will die

POPULAR SONG:
"I Don't Want to Set the
World on Fire"

1942

FILM:
The Man Who Came to Dinner

1945

GERMANY
FEB 13 and Valentine's day
Dresden bombed by Allies,
over 30,000 killed

U.S.A.
AUG 6
Drops atomic bomb on Hiroshima.
80,000 killed and
people at epicenter vaporized

MAY 7
Germany surrenders

MAY 8 VE (Victory in Europe) Day

Death camps, where 6 million jews,
gypsies, homosexuals and other
targeted groups were killed
discovered by Allied troops

AUG 15
JAPAN
VJ (Victory in Japan) Day
Japan surrenders

ENOLA GAY

"BIG BABY" EXPLODES OVER HIROSHIMA

IT IS NOT UNTIL 1945, AFTER THE ATOMIC BOMBS ARE DROPPED ON NAGASAKI AND HIROSHIMA, THAT THE JAPANESE CONCEDE DEFEAT...

...the same year Bobbie marries a Japanese woman... another triumph of LOVE over HISTORY!

MARGE
(Japanese/American)

BOBBIE
(Chinese/Austrian)

SAM AND POLDI ARE APPALLED

"MY DAD WAS AGAINST ME MARRYING ANYONE OF JAPANESE BLOOD..."

FRANK LONG
(BOBBIE)

MARGE LONG

"YES, THE JAPANESE WERE ALL BEING SENT BACK, BUT I DIDN'T WANT TO GO, AND I SAID I WAS GOING TO MARRY FRANK. MY DAD SAID IT WAS OKAY, BUT MY MOTHER WAS A BIT... CONCERNED."

MARGE'S DAD WAS THE MIXED-RACE AMERICAN SIDE. HER MOTHER WAS MIXED-RACE FROM JAPAN... DIFFERENT EXPERIENCES!

"Then the roof almost fell in. God! They (Sam and Poldi) were just dumbfounded. They just didn't want to talk to me anymore. They were just, "We're finished! We're finished!" I said, "Okay, if you feel that way...."

SO, SAM CUTS OFF TIES WITH HIS SON. HE AND POLDI ARE ALONE.

WELL, NOT QUITE ALONE... NEESA AND HER HUSBAND, N.C., ARE STILL IN SHANGHAI.... BUT SOMETHING ELSE IS JUST ON THE HORIZON.

MAO, SALUTING TANKS AND TROOPS

THE COMMUNIST REVOLUTIONARY ARMY IS COMING!

133

After years of civil war, the Communists under Mao Tse Tung have a special vendetta against Shanghai because of its association with the losing side of that exchange....

CHAIRMAN MAO TSE TUNG

CHIANG KAI-SHEK

...especially with the Republican General, Chiang Kai-shek, who fled to Formosa (Taiwan) to continue his fight.

Sam and Poldi leave China in 1948, just in front of the Communist Revolution. Sam's theatres are taken over. Everything seems to be lost. They sail for America...

...via Hong Kong, on the way reconciling with their other married children. The wars and conflicts have given everybody an opportunity to reconsider their priorities. They want to be part of their family.

"SO, WE SAID, 'HOW ABOUT COMING TO OUR PLACE AND STAYING THE NIGHT WITH US, BECAUSE WE HAVE NICE, SOFT BEDS.' BECAUSE THEY (SAM & POLDI) WERE ALWAYS COMPLAINING ABOUT THE BEDS IN HONG KONG, THAT THEY WERE SO HARD. SO, THEY SAID, 'OKAY, WE'LL COME OVER.' SO, THEY SLEPT IN OUR BEDS AND WE SLEPT IN THE LIVINGROOM. AND THE NEXT MORNING THEY SAID, 'OH, WHAT A LOVELY SLEEP WE HAD.' EVERYTHING WAS FINE. AND THAT'S HOW IT ENDED. EVERYTHING WENT WELL."

My darling Mina,

I received your Father's Day card today. Sorry I did not answer you sooner...

Write me once in a while. I shall be very happy to hear from you. You children have a wonderful mother. Follow her example and save your money for a rainy day...

Do get in touch with your brother once a week. Remember, blood is thicker than water.

Your loving father,

Papa

*Excerpts from a letter Long Tack Sam wrote to his daughter, Mina, after he left Hong Kong for the U.S.A.

POLDI (NEESA) AND N.C. ELECT TO STAY IN SHANGHAI. IN FACT, THEY ARE GRANTED A LOT OF FREEDOM UNDER THE NEW COMMUNIST GOVERNMENT. N.C.'S FAMILY OWNS CEMENT FACTORIES AND THESE ARE NEEDED TO REBUILD THE NEW CHINESE NATION. THEY EVEN HAVE TRAVEL VISAS.

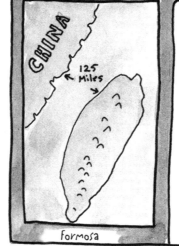

CHINA
125 Miles
Formosa

UNFORTUNATELY, THEY CHOOSE TO TRAVEL TO THE ISLAND OF FORMOSA (NOW TAIWAN), STRONGHOLD OF CHIANG KAI-SHEK, AS HIS GUESTS. THIS PUT THEM IN A BIT OF A PICKLE BACK HOME AND THEY WERE FORCED TO FLEE—LEAVING THEIR FORTUNES BEHIND.

LONG TACK SAM IN ROCKEFELLER CENTER, 1949

LANDING IN NEW YORK CITY, LONG TACK SAM IS GRANTED REFUGEE STATUS, AND THEN AMERICAN CITIZENSHIP... BUT NOT POLDI. EVEN THOUGH SHE HAS CARRIED A CHINESE PASSPORT FOR 40 YEARS, SHE IS STILL CONSIDERED AN AUSTRIAN NATIONAL. SINCE THE U.S. IS NOT AT WAR WITH AUSTRIA ANYMORE, AND AUSTRIA IS NOT IN DANGER OF BEING TAKEN OVER BY COMMUNISTS—THE U.S. DOESN'T WANT HER. SHE HAS TO KEEP GOING TO CANADA TO RENEW HER VISITOR'S VISA.

I SPENT A COUPLE OF YEARS IN CHICAGO, AND IT WAS ALWAYS VERY STRESSFUL RENEWING MY OWN VISA. WOULD THEY LET ME IN THIS YEAR? WAS I STILL ELIGIBLE? DID THEY LIKE ME? AND THIS WAS WAY BEFORE SEPT. 11, 2001, WHEN EVERYTHING GOT A LOT MORE COMPLICATED FOR EVERYONE.

THE UNITED STATES HAS ALWAYS BEEN A SYMBOL OF ACCEPTANCE OF PEOPLE FROM ALL OVER THE WORLD... BUT IT HAS NEVER BEEN EASY TO ACTUALLY MOVE THERE. NOT FOR MOST PEOPLE.

AMERICA IS REMARKABLY UNTOUCHED BY THE WAR, WHILE THE REST OF THE WORLD LIES IN RUBBLE.

1950
KOREA
war breaks out

POPULAR SONG:
"Mona Lisa" recorded by
Nat King Cole

SAM, RETIRED AS A MAGICIAN, SEEMS TO HAVE NO PROBLEM FILLING HIS TIME WITH CLUBS AND SECRET SOCIETIES OF ALL KINDS. HE'S A MEMBER OF THE GRAND ORDER OF THE WATER RATS, THE VAUDEVILLE CLUB, THE INTERNATIONAL BROTHERHOOD OF MAGIC...

....AND, ODDLY ENOUGH, HE IS A 32 DEGREE MASON. HERE HE IS, WITH A GROUP OF OTHER ASIAN MASONS INFRONT OF A MAP CONNECTING ASIA TO AMERICA. MAKING CONNECTIONS WAS WHAT SAM'S LIFE HAD ALWAYS BEEN ABOUT. (LOOK AT THEIR FEZZES. THESE MEN ARE SHRINERS*.)

*Ancient Arabic Order of the Nobles of the Mystic Shrine sponsor circuses and hospitals and other charitiable works, especially for children.

SAM AND POLDI LIVED ON 72ND STREET IN NEW YORK CITY AT THE RUXTON HOTEL. FINALLY, I GET TO THE PART OF THEIR LIVES THAT MY MOTHER AND HER SIBLINGS KNOW SOMETHING ABOUT

Ruxton Hotel

ROSEMARY FLEMING, PIANIST
MINA'S DAUGHTER

"THEY LIVED IN A SMALL APARTMENT. THEY WERE THERE FOR MANY YEARS. AND WE SPENT AT LEAST THREE CHRISTMASES WITH THEM."

EVEN IF THEY DISAGREED ON THE ODD DETAIL... MEMORY IS LIKE THAT.

YOU WENT EVERY CHRISTMAS?

VIVIEN STACKPOLE, BALLET DANCER
MINA'S DAUGHTER

"NO, JUST ONCE. AND WE STAYED WITH THEM. IT WAS FUN."

1952

ENGLAND
George VI dies

ARGENTINA
Evita, (charismatic wife of labor
president Juan Peron) dies

MIDDLE EAST
School-aged Crown Prince Hussein
becomes King of Jordan

FILM:
3-D movies—*Bwana Devil*
promises "a lion in your lap"

POPULAR SONG:
"I Saw Mommy Kissing Santa Claus"

1953

ENGLAND
Queen Elizabeth II crowned

POPULAR SONG:
"The Happy Wanderer"
"Cry Me a River"

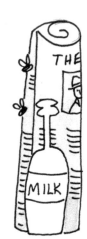

FRED TO, INVENTOR
MINA'S SON

"THEY WOULD SEND ME DOWN IN THE MORNING FOR A BIT OF MILK OR NEWSPAPER OR SOMETHING."

"GRANDPA USED TO LOVE TO STAY UP LATE AND WATCH WRESTLING MATCHES IN THE EVENINGS."

"HE WAS JUST SUCH A NICE MAN, YOU KNOW. SO GOOD TO CHILDREN... TO US, ANYWAY..."

"...AND HE ALWAYS PLAYED WITH HIS BUDGERIGAR..."

140

"...AND GRANDMA USED TO USE OUR SHAMPOO. THAT WAS WHEN SHAMPOO FIRST CAME OUT IN A TUBE. SHE THOUGHT IT WAS TOOTHPASTE.

SHE CAME OUT FOAMING AND SAID,

'HOW COME YOUR TOOTHPASTE FOAMS SO MUCH?' THAT WAS FUNNY."

YOU WERE HOW OLD?

"14, 15... ROSEMARY WAS A LITTLE OLDER..."

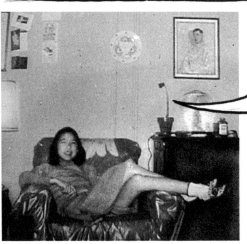

"SHE ALWAYS TOOK US SHOPPING TO MACY'S BASEMENT SALES..."

Poldi, with Rosemary, Fred and Vivien, Christmas 1953.

LINDA TRECEK, TEACHER
NEESA'S DAUGHTER

JAN LONG, ADMINISTRATOR
NEESA'S SON

NEESA AND N.C. HAD ALSO MIGRATED TO THE U.S. AND LIVED IN NEW JERSEY. THEIR CHILDREN, JAN AND LINDA, LIVE IN CALIFORNIA. THEY DIDN'T KNOW A LOT ABOUT THEIR GRANDPARENTS, BUT LINDA HAD FABULOUS PHOTOS HIDDEN UNDER HER BED THAT HELPED ME PUT THIS WHOLE STORY TOGETHER.

Jan & Linda with Sam & Poldi

IT LOOKED LIKE A NICE TIME IN THEIR LIVES. THEY STILL SEEMED VERY MUCH IN LOVE.

(Even though Poldi complained a lot about Sam's driving. Everybody told me THAT story!)

FISHIN'

SWIMMIN'

FROM TIME TO TIME, SAM WOULD BE COERCED OUT OF RETIREMENT FOR A SPECIAL PERFORMANCE FOR MAGICIAN'S BENEFITS...

OLD VAUDEVILLE
HANDS WERE
ALWAYS
DROPPING BY
SAM AND
POLDI'S TINY
RUXTON FLAT,

KEEPING EACH
OTHER UP ON
THE LATEST
CLOSE-UP
MAGIC TRICKS

AND RELIVING
STORIES OF THE
<u>OLD DAYS</u>

NOVEMBER, 1930 · 30 Cents a Copy

THE · SPHINX
AN INDEPENDENT MAGAZINE FOR MAGICIANS

LONG TACK SAM, THE GREATEST OF THE CHINESE MAGICIANS AND CALLED BY THE PRESIDENT OF CHINA A TRUE AMBASSADOR OF HIS COUNTRY. HE IS ABOUT TO LEAVE FOR A TOUR OF AUSTRALIA AND NEW ZEALAND.

A COMPLETE WRIGHT AND LARSEN MANUSCRIPT ON MINDREADING IN THIS ISSUE. ARTICLES AND TRICKS BY DOWNS, HILLIAR, ROUCLERE, WILFRED JONSON, HAHNE AND BERG, AND MANY OTHERS. TWENTY NEW EFFECTS.

OFFICIAL ORGAN : SOCIETY of AMERICAN MAGICIANS

VOL. XXIX, No. 9

SAM IS FINALLY MAGIC ROYALTY, AND EVERY MAGICIAN OF HIS TIME REVERED HIM. EVERYBODY KNEW HIM...

ORSON WELLES

"I HAD OTHER TEACHERS, INCLUDING THE GREAT LONG TACK SAM."*
(*from the BBC's Orson Welles *Sketchbook* 1955)

This is Jackie Flosso, magician and heir to Flosso Hornmann magic shop. Every magician in town passes through here.

JACK FLOSSO
MAGICIAN

"THE LAST TIME I SAW LONG TACK SAM, IT WAS AT A SOCIETY OF AMERICAN MAGICIANS BENEFIT AT THE ROXY THEATER IN NEW YORK CITY.

THE ROXY IS NOW A T.G.I. FRIDAYS

JACKIE: "He looked wonderful! He looked very youthful onstage and did his entire act that he'd done years before. And it was an Oriental review, and they had all Chinese performers in the show.
He was the master of ceremonies in an all-Chinese review."

*To the left are 3D images, not film stills, created by Nathaniel Akin

Sam performed the "Linking Rings", an old Chinese standard

LIKO PANG
MAGICIAN

"TO ME, IT'S NOT OLD-FASHIONED. I CALL IT A CLASSIC OF MAGIC. I LOVE THE LINKING RINGS!"

"HE DID MANY WONDERFUL EFFECTS, INCLUDING THE SOMERSAULT, WHERE HE PRODUCES A BOWL OF WATER."

HE STILL DID THE GOLDFISH BOWL TRICK. HE WAS 73 YEARS OLD!!

148

LET ME DIVULGE A MAGIC SECRET...
HOW YOU DO THE GOLDFISH BOWL TRICK

1 Take a 15-20 lb bowl
and fill it with water
and goldfish

2 Sling it between your
legs, hidden, under
your clothes

3 Do a forward roll

Stand up, and reveal it from underneath
a silk scarf you are waving around.

*In the old days, someone would bang
on a gong. This served as the musical
accompaniment when there were no
musicians to be had. Sam would say the
magic words, "I kong, I kalong dong,"
which means absolutely nothing, but
added to the drama!

SIMPLE!

73 YEARS
OLD!

INSANE!

BUT WARS AND REVOLUTIONS AND AN EXTREMELY <u>LONG</u> RETIREMENT DWINDLED HIS FORTUNES AWAY, DESPITE POLDI'S FRUGAL WAYS...

"IN THE 50'S, CHINA HAD A SPECIAL DEAL WITH AMERICAN CITIZENS SO THEY COULD BE COMPENSATED FOR THEIR PROPERTY THAT HAD BEEN TAKEN OVER BY THE STATE. WHEN I ASKED MY DAD ABOUT WHERE HIS DOCUMENTS WERE FOR THE THEATRES, HE SAID, 'I THREW THEM ALL AWAY. I THOUGHT THEY WERE GONE FOREVER.'"

150

TO-NIGHT'S PROGRAMME

The Oriental Master of Magic

LONG TACK SAM

Supported by his Entire

COMPANY OF CHINESE ARTISTS

and the

CREAM OF EUROPE'S VAUDEVILLE STARS.

Wright & Jaques, Ltd., Printers.

HAD THEY STAYED IN NEW YORK CITY, MAYBE SAM WOULD HAVE BEEN REMEMBERED, AT LEAST IN THE ANNALS OF AMERICAN ENTERTAINMENT...

BUT SAM AND POLDI WERE IN A TRAFFIC ACCIDENT. THEY WERE BOTH STRUCK BY A MOTORCYCLE...

Sam & Poldi on an ocean liner, on their way back to Europe

HE AND POLDI RETIRED TO THEIR VILLA IN AUSTRIA.

VILLA LONG

They went back to Austria to convalesce

ONE NIGHT, LONG WENT TO BED WITH A HEATING PAD.

THE PAD BURNED HIM AND HE JUMPED OUT OF BED BREAKING HIS LEG.

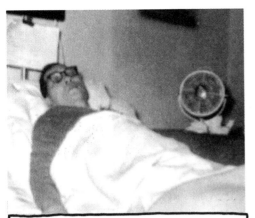

In the hospital, Sam develops gangrene.

Bobbie said: "They didn't look after the infection. It didn't have to be that way."

Our old friend, Long Tack Sam, is convalescing in the hospital and would love to hear from friends in America.

Please write...

Personal, in *The Linking Ring*

✝

WITH DEEPEST SORROW WE ANNOUNCE
THE DEATH OF OUR
DEARLY BELOVED HUSBAND AND FATHER

LONG TACK SAM

WHO PASSED AWAY IN LINZ, AUSTRIA, ON AUGUST 7, 1961, AFTER A LONG ILLNESS IN HIS 76TH YEAR.

POLDI LONG
WIFE

MRS. ERNEST TO
MRS. NEESA LONG YAO
DAUGHTERS

MR. FRANK LONG
SON

„VILLA LONG", LINZ, AUGUST 14, 1961

IN THE OLD CEMETARY IN LINZ IS THE TOMBSTONE OF LONG TACK SAM... AND POLDI... WHO WENT MAD WITH GRIEF AND DIED, A YEAR AFTER HIS DEATH, IN A SANITORIUM IN VIENNA.

THERE'S NO ONE LEFT WHO TENDS THEIR GRAVES

It is not just Long Tack Sam and Poldi who are gone, it's their children, their show, their entire history.

A LOT OF THE MAGICIANS AND OTHER PEOPLE THAT I MET WHILE TRYING TO RESEARCH SAM'S STORY HAVE PASSED ALONG NOW, TOO...

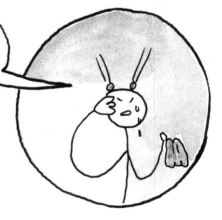

JACKIE FLOSSO   LIKO PANG

JOHN BOOTH   SUN TAI

JAY MARSHALL   ELAINE LUND

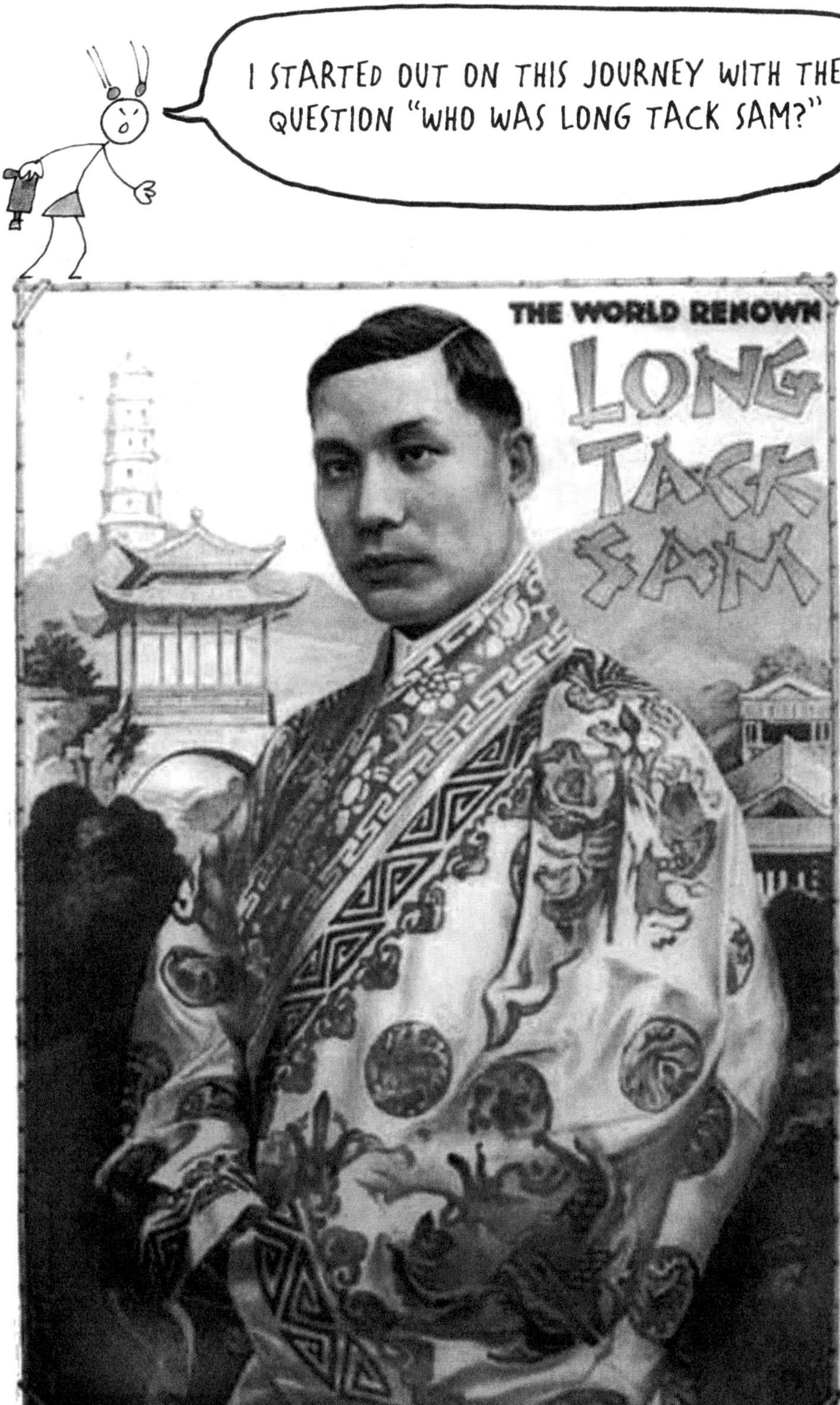
I STARTED OUT ON THIS JOURNEY WITH THE QUESTION "WHO WAS LONG TACK SAM?"
THE WORLD RENOWN
LONG TACK SAM

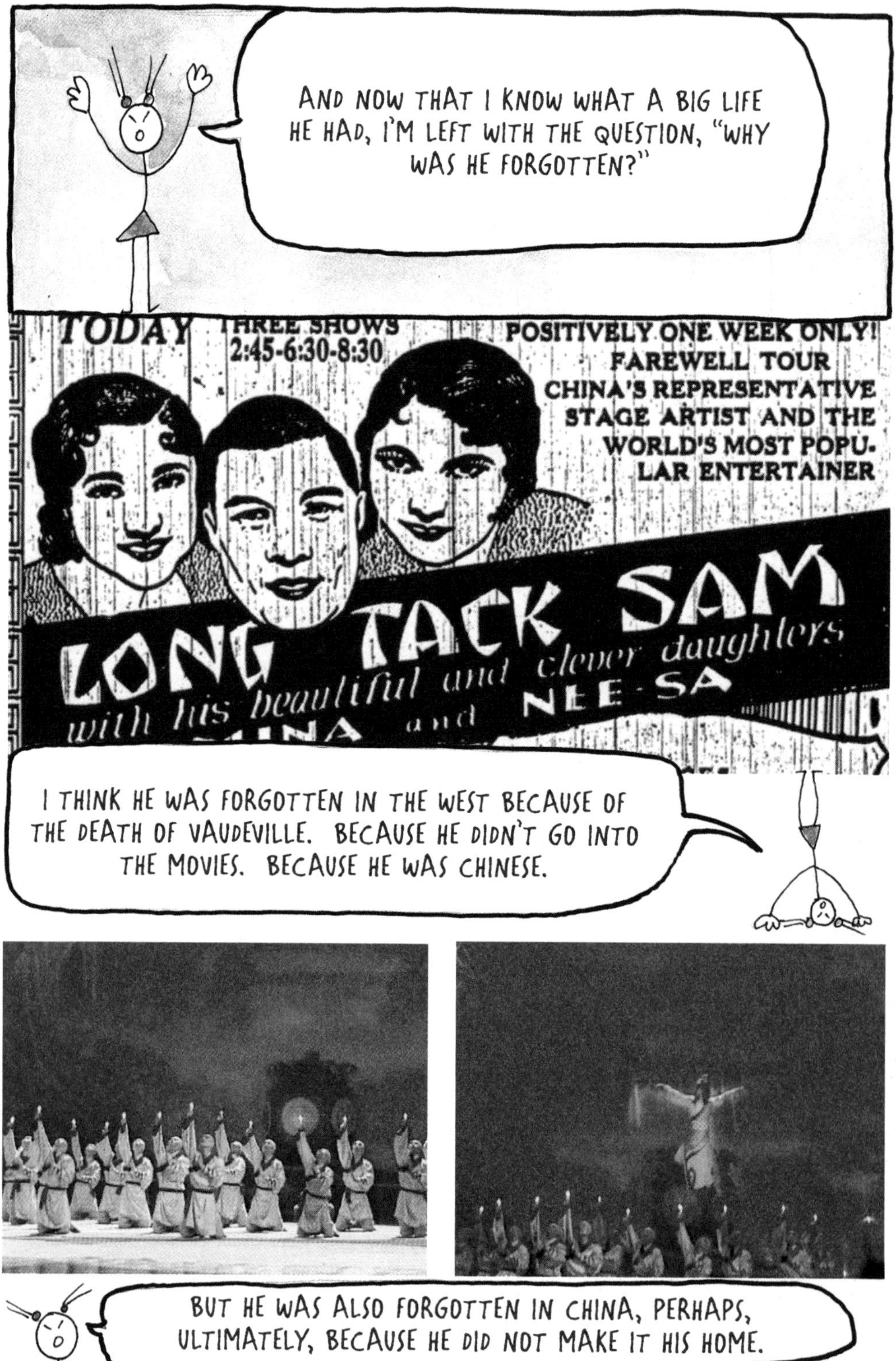
AND NOW THAT I KNOW WHAT A BIG LIFE HE HAD, I'M LEFT WITH THE QUESTION, "WHY WAS HE FORGOTTEN?"
TODAY
THREE SHOWS 2:45-6:30-8:30
POSITIVELY ONE WEEK ONLY! FAREWELL TOUR CHINA'S REPRESENTATIVE STAGE ARTIST AND THE WORLD'S MOST POPULAR ENTERTAINER
LONG TACK SAM
with his beautiful and clever daughters
and
NEE-SA
I THINK HE WAS FORGOTTEN IN THE WEST BECAUSE OF THE DEATH OF VAUDEVILLE. BECAUSE HE DIDN'T GO INTO THE MOVIES. BECAUSE HE WAS CHINESE.
BUT HE WAS ALSO FORGOTTEN IN CHINA, PERHAPS, ULTIMATELY, BECAUSE HE DID NOT MAKE IT HIS HOME.

BUT WHAT PUZZLES ME IS WHY HE WAS
FORGOTTEN BY HIS OWN FAMILY.
(OKAY, WE DID CELEBRATE HIS BIRTHDAY,
HIS DEATH DAY AND HIS ANNIVERSARY,
IN GOOD CHINESE STYLE—WHILE GRANNY
WAS STILL ALIVE—BUT WE KNEW NOTHING
ABOUT HIS ACCOMPLISHMENTS).
IS IT A SHOW BUSINESS THING?
(YES, CHILDREN OF SHOW BUSINESS PARENTS
ARE OFTEN RESENTFUL.)
IS IT AN IMMIGRANT THING?
(YES, IMMIGRANTS OFTEN DON'T TAKE
THEIR OLD STORIES INTO THEIR NEW LIVES.)
IS IT BECAUSE WE ALL KEEP MOVING,
KEEP BUSY?
(YES, THAT, TOO!)
MAYBE WE JUST WEREN'T LISTENING!

DISTANCES AND DIFFERENCES KEEP US APART, AND WE FORGET TO REMIND EACH OTHER OF OUR OWN STORIES

I FINISHED MY FILM, AND I SHOWED IT ALL OVER THE WORLD... UNWITTINGLY FOLLOWING SAM'S VAUDEVILLE FOOTSTEPS... THE FILM FESTIVAL CIRCUIT HITS ALL THE SAME PLACES. I MET PEOPLE AT EACH SCREENING WHO KNEW A LITTLE BIT MORE ABOUT THE STORY

THERE HE WAS! LONG TACK SAM, ONSTAGE AGAIN... IN MANY OF THE SAME PLACES HE'D PLAYED WHEN HE WAS A STAR!

AND MY FAMILY CAME OUT TO SEE THE FILM, AND SOMETIMES, TO MEET EACH OTHER FOR THE FIRST TIME.

SAN FRANCISCO   MAR DEL PLATA   TORONTO

SAN DIEGO   SAN JOSE   NEW YORK CITY

MUMBAI

VANCOUVER   HONG KONG

SANTA CRUZ   SINGAPORE

PORTLAND   CLEVELAND   HONOLULU   WASHINGTON, D.C.

LONG TACK SAM — POLDI

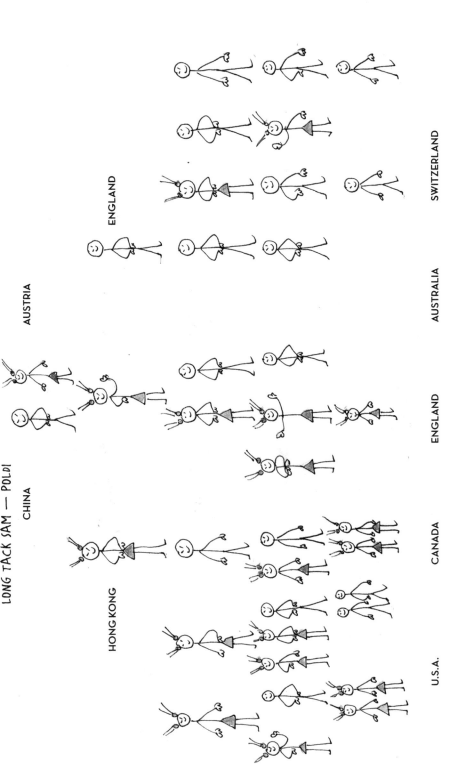

CHINA

AUSTRIA

ENGLAND

SWITZERLAND

AUSTRALIA

HONG KONG

ENGLAND

CANADA

U.S.A.

159

MEMORY IS A LOT LIKE MAGIC. SUDDENLY, WE COULD ALL SEE WHAT WE HAD IN COMMON WITH EACH OTHER. SOMETHING TO CELEBRATE!

...AND I STARTED TO SEE WHAT I HAD IN COMMON WITH MY <u>GREAT</u>-GRANDFATHER... A LEGACY, SO TO SPEAK...

Short hair again →

I'M A FILMMAKER AND AN ANIMATOR.

THE FIRST FILMS WERE ANIMATED—COLLABORATIONS BETWEEN MAGICIANS AND PHOTOGRAPHERS.

* image from
Voyage to the Moon
George Mèliés

I'VE TRAVELLED ALL OVER THE WORLD TRYING TO MAKE MY WORK AND TELL HIS STORY. AND SOMETIMES... IT'S VERY HARD.

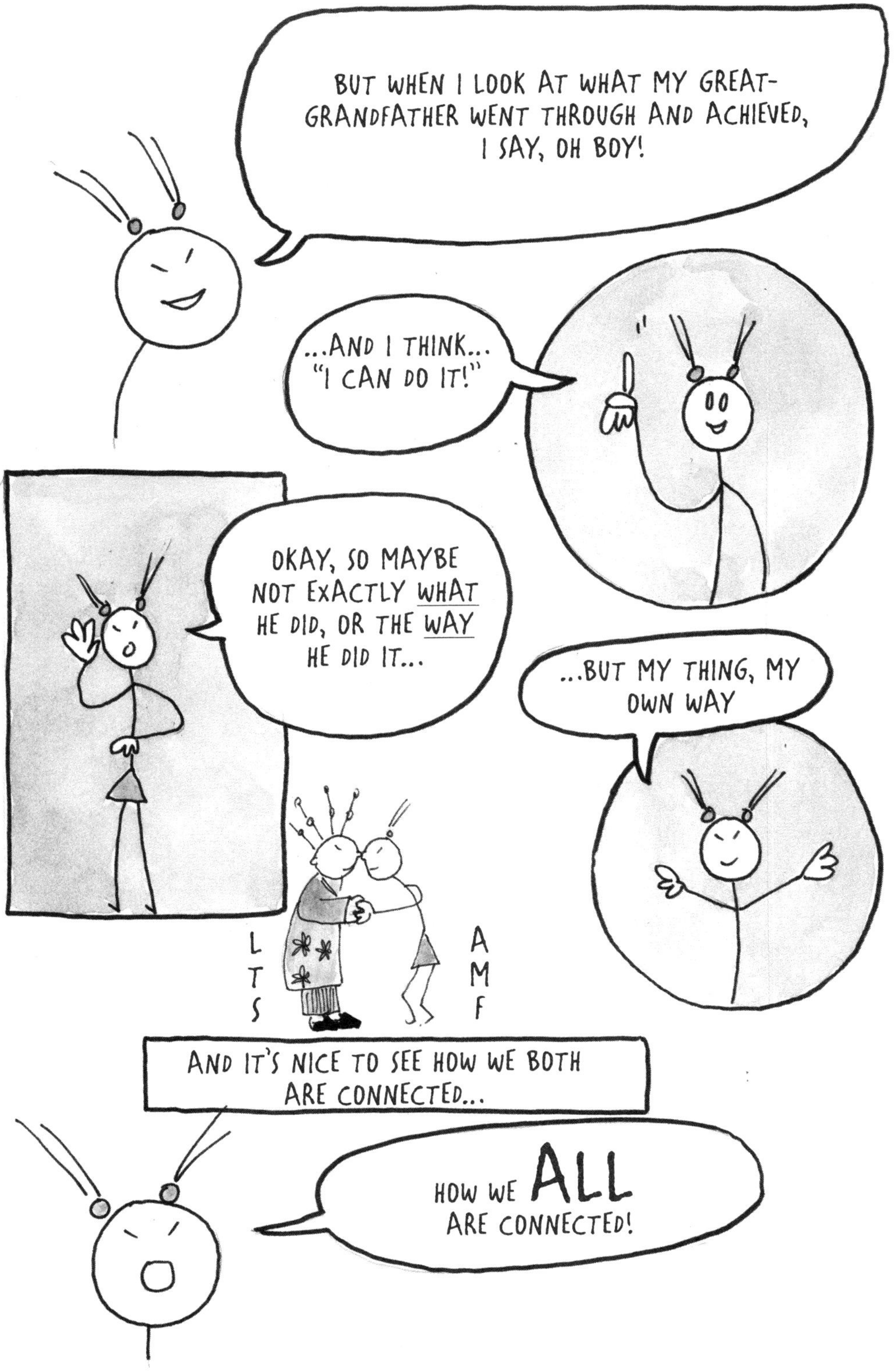
BUT WHEN I LOOK AT WHAT MY GREAT-GRANDFATHER WENT THROUGH AND ACHIEVED, I SAY, OH BOY!
...AND I THINK... "I CAN DO IT!"
OKAY, SO MAYBE NOT EXACTLY WHAT HE DID, OR THE WAY HE DID IT...
...BUT MY THING, MY OWN WAY
LTS
AMF
AND IT'S NICE TO SEE HOW WE BOTH ARE CONNECTED...
HOW WE ALL ARE CONNECTED!

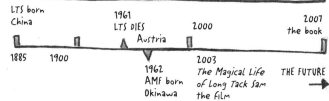

1962

U.S./U.S.S.R.
Cuban Missile Crisis

U.S.A
Marilyn Monroe dies

ART:
Andy Warhol's
Campbell's Soup Cans

Roy Lichtenstein's comic paintings
revolutionize the art world

1963

U.S.S.R.
Cosmonaut Valentina Tereshkova
first woman in space

U.S.A
President Kennedy assassinated
in Dallas

POPULAR SONG:
"Love Me Do" The Beatles' first hit

1964

SOUTH AFRICA
Nelson Mandela imprisoned

POPULAR SONG:
"The Times They Are A-Changin'",
Bob Dylan

"A Love Supreme", John Coltrane

Simon & Garfunkel, first group
to use "ethnic" names in U.S. pop

1965

INDIA
Indira Gandhi elected first
female prime minister

U.S.A.
Sends first ground troops to Vietnam

POPULAR SONG:
"Downtown", Petula Clark

Phrase "flower power" coined

FASHION:
Mary Quant invents miniskirt

1966

CHINA
Cultural Revolution begins

MUSIC:
John Lennon receives death threats
for saying the Beatles are
"bigger than Jesus"

1967

MIDDLE EAST
6 Day War,
Israel annexes West Bank,
Golan Heights

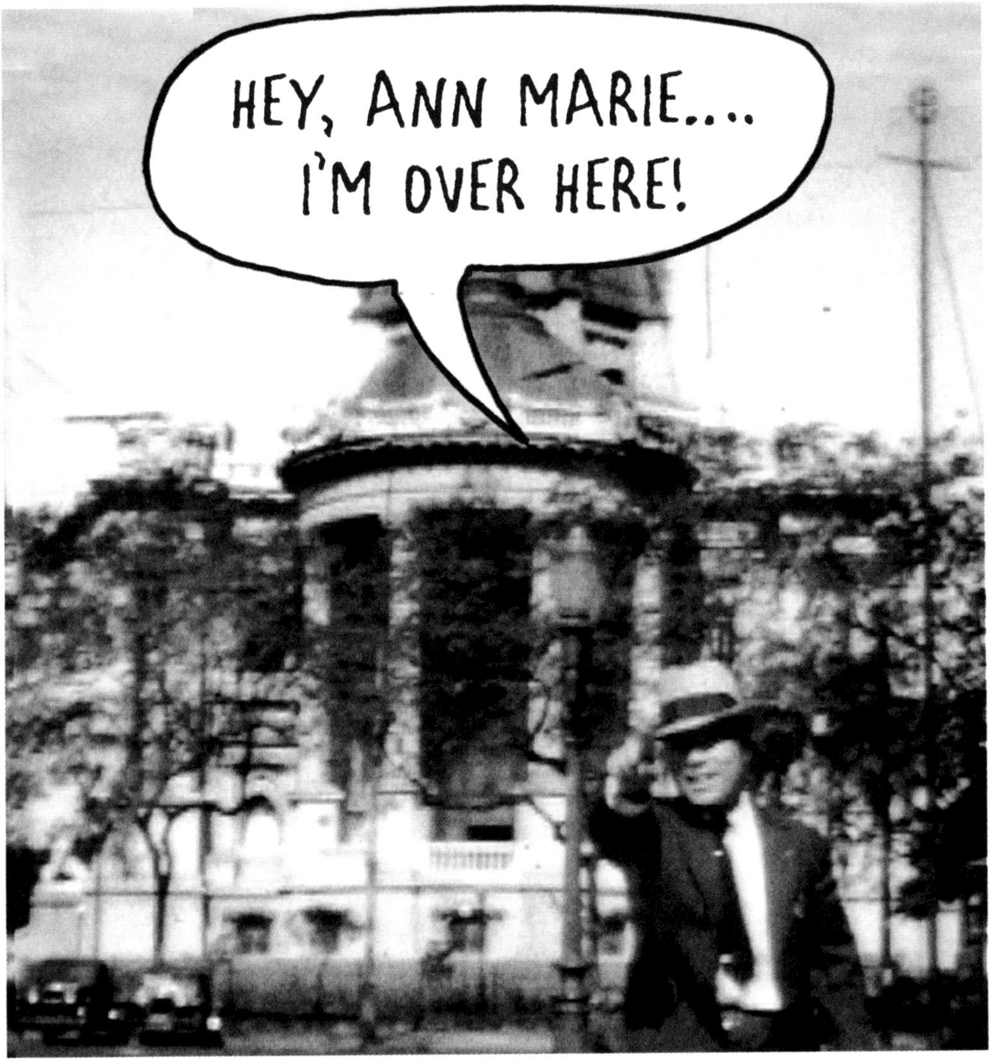
HEY, ANN MARIE....
I'M OVER HERE!

END

Author's Notes

Several years ago, when I began researching the life of my great-grandfather, Long Tack Sam, I thought I would just be filling in a bit of family history. I didn't know much about him, just that he was a vaudevillian magician and did some coin tricks. As a filmmaker who often dabbles in biography and identity, and an immigrant to North America myself, I thought that it would make an interesting contribution to the usual stories of Chinese migration experiences you usually hear about: indentured workers, coolies, the railroad, the laundry, the restaurants. I thought this would present an alternate history, of glamor, entertainment and success. It became much more than that.

Being mixed-race, part of the diaspora of many cultures, really, I am always interested in people's histories and choices. Sam married an Austrian woman in 1908. How did that happen? When I found out that he was a world-famous, globe-hopping magician AND acrobat, I started to wonder, "Why has be been forgotten?"

The resulting film and book trace that journey, both his and mine. I got to revisit almost the entire 20th century through the prism of this one particular man's life, recontextualize world events and see familial patterns and connections throughout the generations that had never really occurred to me at all.

But how to begin? I started off knowing very little about magic, or vaudeville, or my great grandfather, but picked up *Continuous Performance*, Carrie Baliban's biography of her husband A. J. Baliban, who was a theatre impresario and friend of Long Tack Sam's. At the back of the book were lists of world events and popular culture, year by year. This was how I was going to find Sam's life, by making a grid of songs, movies, political events, and the few places and play dates I knew about his life and his show, and fill in the blanks by deduction. Then, the long, forensic process of proving them to be true. We are all affected by the geopolitics of

our own time. Some of our smallest decisions are affected by global events, and have wide-reaching ramifications, whether we realize it or not. That's why I have a timeline of world events that runs through this book, in the margins, to contextualize Sam's life. Sometimes, events directly affected him. Sometimes, happenings in other parts of the world were so radically different, you can't believe they are happening at the same time on the same planet. Look at what's happening now!

When the film came out, my editor, Megan Lynch, saw it on the Sundance Channel and contacted me, asking me if I wanted to adapt it into a graphic novel. I was thrilled but found it surprisingly difficult to translate it into a 2D medium. So much of the flavor and tone and subtext of the film, (which is essentially a giant collage/scrapbook) was in its sound and music and movement, especially the animation (nearly all of the illustrations and photographs were animated). I take you through the film, as narrator, and every inflection and pause is a comment. How to do that in the text of a graphic novel? I hope that I have come up with solutions that do the film and the subject justice. Flip the bottom corner of the book to see an animated sequence from the movie. I used another film character of mine, Stickgirl, to take us through the story.

I want to thank all the artists and magicians and historians and vaudevillians and family and friends who helped me make these works, and a special thanks to Long Tack Sam, who just wouldn't go away and insisted that his story be told. In his specific tale is a common story of humanity. Especially for all of us who, somewhere along the line, made the movement from one part of the world to another for all of those myriad reasons: love, money, war, adventure, famine. Whether we ran from, ran to, or were bought, sold or pulled or seduced, we have a story. And that history shapes our future. Thank you for taking the time to look at this book. Hopefully, it will start a conversation.

1975
POLITICS:
Vietnam war ends

Khmer Rouge march into Phnom Penh, millions will die (Killing Fields)

POPULAR SONG:
"Bohemian Rhapsody", Queen

"Born to Run", Bruce Springsteen

1976
TECHNOLOGY:
Viking brings back first images of Mars

POPULAR SONG:
"Anarchy in the U.K.," Sex Pistols

1977
POLITICS:
"Boat People" flee Vietnam

POPULAR SONG:
"Stayin' Alive," Bee Gees

Elvis Presley dies in Memphis

1978
HEALTH:
Smallpox eradicated

Baby Louise, first test-tube baby, born in U.K.

POPULAR SONG:
"Rock Lobster," B-52's

1979
POPULAR SONG:
"London Calling," The Clash

1980
NATURE:
Mt. St. Helen's erupts

MIDDLE EAST
Iran-Iraq War escalates

Anwar Sadat of Egypt assassinated

1983

POPULAR SONG:
"Billie Jean," Michael Jackson

1984

AFRICA
Famine in Ethiopia

NATURE:
Scientists warn of "global warming"

HEALTH:
H.I.V., the virus that causes
AIDS, is discovered

POPULAR SONG:
"Pride (In the Name of Love)," U2

1985

TECHNOLOGY:
Mobile phones launched in Europe

1986

TECHNOLOGY:
Space shuttle *Challenger*
explodes after take-off

POPULAR SONG:
"We Are The World,"
U.S.A. for Africa

"That's What Friends are For,"
Dione Warwick and Friends

"Walk This Way,"
Run DMC & Aerosmith

1987

POLITICS:
President Reagan and Premier
Gorbachev sign nuclear treaty

NATURE:
Bangladesh hit by catastrophic floods

1988

NATURE:
45,000 die in earthquake
in Armenia

POPULAR SONG:
"Don't Worry, Be Happy,"
Bobby McFerrin

Acknowledgments

This book and its preceding film could not have been completed without the help of many people, some of whom I'd like to mention here. I'd like to thank the Canada Council for the Arts, The National Film Board of Canada, the British Columbia Arts Council and Bruce Alcock for their support of the film. I'd like to thank my editor, Megan Lynch and Riverhead Books for making this illustrated memoir possible, and to gratefully acknowledge the following people/organizations for permission to use their images, stories and artistry.

LONG TACK SAM'S FRIENDS AND FAMILY

Arthur Dearn, Rosemary & Sandy Fleming, Badonna Kahn, Ernst Kriechbaum, Jan Long, Frank Long, Marg Long, Ruby Li Long, Martha Pellegrini, Karen Stackpole, Vivien & Hank Stackpole, Fred To, Ernest & Mina To, Linda Trecek, Leila Venewitz, N.W.Yao.

MAGICIANS, HISTORIANS, ACROBATS, STORYTELLERS

Gordon Bean (Magic Castle), David Ben, Roger Bernheim (Magic Circle), Peter Blanchard, John Nicholls Booth, John Brown (IBM), Patric Caird, David Callahan (New York Public Library), Peggy Case, Maureen Christopher, Edwin A. Dawes, Arthur Dong, Jackie Flosso, Tim Glander, Jay Gorham (S.A.M. Film & Tape Library), Tom House (Ohio Historical Society), Ricky Jay, Elizabeth Johnston (Museum of Anthropology), Dave Kehr, Ben Kim (Chicago Asian Film Festival), Liang-Na (translator), Lu Yi (School for the Circus Arts), Elaine Lund (American Museum of Magic), Jay Marshall (Magic Inc.), Gene Matsuuda, Bill McIlhany, Mark Mitton, James Moy, Norm Nielsen (Nielsen Magic), Stanley Palm, Ileana Pietrobruno, Michael Perovich, David Price Jr. (Egyptian Hall Museum), Jonathan Rosenbaum, Caroline Sisneros (Louis B. Meyer Library), Sun Tai, Marjorie Tom, Ruth Vincent, Wang Feng (Shanghai Acrobatic Troupe), Bart Whaley, Lethiea Wong, Meir Yedid (Magic Times), Zhang Xiao, Zhang YuLin (China Film Archive).

FILM FOOTAGE STILLS
BBC Worldwide Americas, Budget Films, Streamline Films, Long Tack Sam Clan footage, Otto Messmer's and Pat Sullivan's "Felix the Cat in Hollywood," 1923 (courtesy of Don Oriolo) and my own footage.

ANIMATORS and ILLUSTRATORS
Nathaniel Akin, Bruce Alcock, Hannah Cho, Ted Dave, Hilary Denny, Iain Gardner, Ian Godfrey, Julian Lawrence, Ceile Prowse, Tim Stuby, Jorge Veloso, Younger Yan.

PHOTOGRAPHERS
Ted Allen (Vidal Studios), Irving Archer, Bloom Studios, Chelsea Studios, Deluxe Studios, De Mirjian Studios, Dietz Studio, Hall & Company, Harsook, Hof Studios, Felix Lehmann, Mitchell, Moody, Maurice Seymour, Strand, Sussman, Joel Yael (Time/Life Pictures), Getty Images, Long Tack Sam's family collection

LAYOUT ARTIST
Josue Menjivar

1989
GERMANY
Berlin Wall comes down

CHINA
Student protests in Tiananmen Square

POPULAR SONG
"Fight The Power," Public Enemy

1990
TECHNOLOGY:
Hubble space telescope launched

POPULAR SONG:
"Nothing Compares 2 U,"
Sinéad O'Connor

1991
U.S.S.R.
Coup topples Gorbachev

POPULAR SONG:
"Losing My Religion," R.E.M.

1992
U.S.A.
Race riots in Los Angeles

POPULAR SONG:
"Smells Like Teen Spirit," Nirvana

1993
U.S.A.
Bomb explodes under World Trade Center

MIDDLE EAST
Israel and PLO sign peace accord in U.S.

POPULAR SONG:
"Man on the Moon," R.E.M.

Prince changes his name to a symbol

1994
EUROPE
Serbian troops bomb Sarajevo

AFRICA
War in Rwanda, Hutu government against Tutsi rebels

Bibliography

Many of the bibliographic references I came across were fragments. In some cases, I have no more information than the periodical itself, but this might pique your interest on your own path of discovery. And I can't begin to tell you the growing usefulness of the Internet from the time I began my research in 1998. The "facts" I found there only reaffirmed my thesis that it's hard to know what is true. Find at least 3 sources that say the same thing (and still cross your fingers that they weren't all quoting from the same material!). Here are some I hope you find useful:

Baliban, Carrie, Continuous Performance, A.J.Baliban Foundation, New York, 1964

Bamberg, David, Illusion Show, Meyerbooks, 1991

Booth, John N., Keys to Magic's Inner World, Ray Goulet's Magic Art Book Company, 1999

Christopher, Milbourne & Maureen, The Illustrated History of Magic, copyright, 1973, Heinemann,1973

Dexter, Will, The Riddle of Ching Ling Soo, Arco Publishers, London, 1955

Goldston, Will, Will Goldston's "Who's Who in Magic", Will Goldston Ltd., Aladdin House

Junior Chronicle of the 20th Century, DK Publishing, 1997

Lee, Anthony W. Picturing Chinatown: Art and Orientalism in San Francisco, U. of California Press, 2001

Moy, James, Marginal Sights—Staging the Chinese in America, University of Iowa Press, 1993

Mulholland, John, John Mulholland's Book of Magic, Charles Scribner's Sons, New York, 1963

Mulholland, John, Quicker than the Eye, Hobbs Merrill, 1932

Price, David, Magic, 1985

Tony Taylor, Spotlight on 101 Great Magic Acts, 1975

www.carygrant.com

PERIODICALS:
Genii Magazine, April 1950
The Linking Ring, Jul/52, Apr/53, Dec/61, June/40, Jan/68
Magic Circle Mirror, July/71
Magician's Monthly
Magicana, Feb/March 99
The Magazine of Magic
The Malayan Magician, Sept/64
The New Tops
The New Yorker, Sept. 3/55
The Sphinx, Nov/30, Oct/30, Dec/32, Apr/50, Apr/51
Variety, 1914-61
LIFE

For more information about the film, go to
www.longtacksam.com.

1998
  U.S.A.
  Lewinsky scandal

  MIDDLE EAST
  Iraq disarmament crisis

  NATURE:
  Yantze River Floods

  Major earthquake in Iraq

  FILM:
  Titanic

  POPULAR SONG:
  "My Heart Will Go On,"
  Celine Dion

1999
  MIDDLE EAST
  Air India flight highjacked
  to Kandahar

  TECHNOLOGY;
  Panic over Y2K

  POPULAR SONG:
  "Smooth," Santana
  featuringRob Thomas

2000
  NATURE:
  Mt. Etna erupts

  POPULAR SONG:
  "I Try," Macy Gray

2001
  U.S.A.
  Terrorists fly planes fly into
  World Trade Center

  POPULAR SONG:
  "Love Don't Cost a Thing,"
  Jennifer Lopez

2002
  NATURE:
  Larsen B Ice Shelf begins disintegrating

  FILM:
  Chicago

  POPULAR SONG:
  "Complicated," Avril Lavigne

Fonts

Litterbox,
Dean Stanton, 1995. Published by Image Club.

Born on a nice sunny Saturday in 1967, in good ol' Calgary, Dean Stanton graduated from the Alberta College of Art and Design in 1990 with a diploma in visual communications, and began a career as an illustrator.

NeutraFace
Christian Schwartz, 2002. Published by House Industries.

Inspired by architect Richard Neutra's designs, Christian Schwartz composed an entire alphabet and added a complementary lowercase which previously did not exist. The final Neutraface Display family includes five weights in regular and alternate variations and a unique titling font.

Source:
Litterbox
Identifont
www.identifont.com

Neutraface
House Industries
www.houseind.com